Additional Praise for *Sticky Learning*

"With a laser focus on the importance of long-term memory formation in student learning, Inglis introduces accessible, brain-wise strategies to help seminary faculty shape focused and memorable learning experiences for their students."

Katherine Turpin
Iliff School of Theology

"*Sticky Learning* provides an engaging mixture of grounded educational psychology, neurobiology, teaching methods, and online resources, all designed to help teachers facilitate learning in the myriad settings from congregational ministry to seminary education. Holly Inglis first moves the reader through a range of constructivist learning theories, anchoring her work in cognitive theorists like Jerome Bruner, Lev Vygotsky, and Howard Gardner. Inglis then unpacks recent insights within neuroscience, explaining both the basic biology of the brain's learning and memory, providing a sound introduction to the neurological basis for educational practice. Throughout the book, Inglis constantly underscores her theory with practical suggestions for facilitating learning, giving concrete examples to help teachers guide learning that 'sticks' with students. Bracketed by the sagely wisdom of experienced educator Roger Nishioka and curriculum innovator Kathy Dawson, Inglis both challenges and inspires educators to a new journey: one that invites educators to embrace innovation, artistry, and the sacramental imagination of co-learning with their students."

Dean G. Blevins
Nazarene Theological Seminary

"Through a carefully crafted and approachable text, Inglis and her colleagues explore the ways we learn, how the brain remembers, and how that should challenge us to reimagine how we teach students and understand multiple learning processes. For anyone interested in conversations about the changing landscape of learning and teaching, Inglis provides a neurological, developmental, and practical conversation through which we can explore the multiple ways to reach students and create meaning in our courses."

Jason C. Whitehead
Iliff School of Theology

"Inglis, Dawson, and Nishioka have collaborated to provide a unique and valuable resource for those who not only 'teach' but who genuinely care about student learning. Informed by and addressed to our fast-changing cultural and pedagogical contexts, *Sticky Learning* draws upon research that many busy seminary professors cannot access—for example, fields such a neuroscience—to provide both insight and strategies for teaching in ways that are truly memorable."

W. David Buschart
Denver Seminary

Sticky Learning

How Neuroscience Supports Teaching That's Remembered

Holly J. Inglis

with

Kathy L. Dawson
Rodger Y. Nishioka

STICKY LEARNING
How Neuroscience Supports Teaching That's Remembered

Cover image: PET Scan of Normal Brain of a Twenty Year Old © Visuals Unlimited/Corbis
Cover design: Laurie Ingram
Book design: PerfecType, Nashville, TN

Library of Congress Cataloging-in-Publication Data is available
Print ISBN: 978-1-4514-8878-4
eBook ISBN: 978-1-4514-8965-1

The paper used in this publication meets the minimum requirements of American National Standard for Information Sciences — Permanence of Paper for Printed Library Materials, ANSI Z329.48-1984.

Manufactured in the U.S.A.

Contents

Part One

Where We Are

Toto, I've a feeling we're not in Kansas anymore.
—Dorothy, *The Wizard of Oz*

Chapter 1

The Changing Landscape

Holly J. Inglis

What's the stickiest thing you can imagine? Maybe it's pine pitch, or wallpaper paste, or duct tape, or a burr in your pets' fur. Have you ever gotten a song or an advertising jingle stuck in your head? Have you ever wondered why that tune won't go away but you can't remember the three things you wanted to get at the grocery store? Why do certain things stick with us either temporarily or over time? Intangible things, like concepts and ideas, can be sticky, too, but what makes one idea sticky and another idea seem to disappear? Since its release in 2007, the book *Made to Stick* has become popular with managers, marketers, teachers, ministers, entrepreneurs, and others who want to make their ideas stick. The authors, Chip and Dan Heath, borrow the concept of "stickiness" from Malcolm Gladwell's popular book, *The Tipping Point*, and apply it as a practical tool to create and construct effective ideas that transform behavior. In *The Tipping Point*, Gladwell argues that the method of presentation and the structure of information greatly affect the "stickiness" of a message. "Stickiness means that a message makes an impact. . . . It sticks in your memory. . . . Unless you remember what I tell you, why would you ever change your behavior?"[1]

---

*QR code URL: http://www.ted.com/talks/sir_ken_robinson_bring_on_the_revolution. Here, creativity expert Sir Ken Robinson makes a case that education does not need reform—it needs a revolution.

1. Malcolm Gladwell, *The Tipping Point: How Little Things Can Make a Big Difference* (Boston: Little, Brown, 2000), 25.

Sticky Learning Is Effective Learning

What is sticky learning?

Every educator wants to believe that he or she can have a lasting impact on students. The greatest impact an instructor can have is not by merely imparting wisdom or knowledge but by understanding how learning occurs and how learning can be reinforced and become part of the long-term memory of the student, having an impact not only on their thinking and reflection in the current setting, but their actions and behavior in settings far beyond the classroom. As professors become more aware of elements of learning and memory and are able to adjust pedagogy and content delivery, they can truly become agents of transformation for their learners. Sticky learning refers to knowledge and methods that may be applied in various contexts to enable your ideas to be understood and remembered, and to have a lasting impact.

Who taught you how to teach?

Recall the last time you were a student in a traditional classroom. What did the room look like? Where was the instructor? Who was in the classroom with you? How was information conveyed or presented? Where was the focal point of the classroom—was it with the professor or the students? What was the primary purpose of the classroom experience—to convey content, to practice skills, to interact with ideas and concepts with other students? How did you feel as a student in that classroom? Was it effective and memorable learning for you?

What is effective learning?

Are there certain educators who are memorable in your own educational experiences? What made them memorable—was it their engaging approach to material in the classroom, their personal interactions with students, their thorough grasp of knowledge or their passion for their field of study? In student evaluations, these professors may have been identified as "great" and their colleagues may have noted them as highly effective. All the students wanted to take their classes. What do you remember from their classes?

What is effective teaching?

Reflect back to the first time you stood before a class as an instructor. How did you know what to do? In some cases, we may choose to model our teaching after a particularly memorable professor or to emulate a respected colleague, but in most instances, we may simply be duplicating the type of learning environment we experienced ourselves. We replicate what we know. Conventional wisdom might suggest that, with some exceptions, of course, the methods and practices we use to craft educational experiences for our students are modeled after the way in which we received our own education and the classrooms in which we gained our knowledge, and will, in turn, become models for our students as they create educational experiences in future ministry settings. We teach as we are taught.

Surveying the Landscape

This book is part exegesis, intended to exegete gently particular elements of the culture of higher education in religious and theological studies. While theological and religious education is unique, it is nevertheless affected by many of the same cultural and economic realities that affect universities and colleges across America. In addition, it is affected by the spiritual and religious realities of our society as well. We must therefore exegete our culture, our students, our teaching, and ourselves in the same way we might approach an exegesis of a difficult text. Today's students face a much different religious, cultural, and economic reality than earlier generations of students. Professors in most theological or religious-studies classrooms were likely socialized in relatively stable social and religious contexts. Many faculty members were likely born into a particular faith tradition with relatively stable religious institutions, pursued a liberal-arts education, and followed a reasonably direct career path. Few students now enjoy such securities. Some arrive with identities formed in the midst of postmodern struggles with fragmentation, broken homes, broken communities, broken churches, and broken worlds. Faculty members from several seminaries across the country were asked to identify hallmarks of students entering their institutions.[2] In addition to noting critical deficiencies in writing, reading, and thinking, their comments included:

- Lack of knowledge of their own religious tradition
- Strong sense of "spiritual but not religious"
- Hyphenated or complex religious identities
- Religious identities that have been formed through dialogue with other religious traditions and options
- Come with little knowledge or experience of the breadth of religion in America
- Less experience in organized religious institutions
- Less understanding of the intersection between faith and life

The Association of Theological Schools reports that slightly over 40 percent of the students enrolled in theological education in 2013 were over forty years old.[3] Theological and religious studies continue to attract older, nontraditional

---

2. Philip Clayton, William B. Lawrence, and Ian McFarland, interview with Fortress Press, Minneapolis, MN, February 2013.

3. Association of Theological Schools, "Annual Institutional Data Tables: Table 2.14-B Head Count Enrollment by Degree Program, Age, and Gender, Fall 2012," http://www.ats.edu/uploads/resources /institutional-data/annual-data-tables/2012-2013-annual-data-tables.pdf.

students, while enrollment for some other age groups appears to be stagnating.[4] Robin Steinke, president of Luther Seminary in St. Paul, Minnesota, says that, "The landscape is certainly changing, but exactly what it is going to look like is still up for grabs. . . . We must be ready to adapt at any time. . . . We must be places where people can gather to share their own wisdom and learn from one another. . . . We have to get more creative and teach our future leaders how to engage [and] how to make complex issues of doctrine and theology engaging."[5]

For more of Dr. Steinke's perspective on the changing landscape, read her Seminarium blogs.[6]

In light of the changing landscape of theological and religious-studies education, this book also functions therapeutically as a mirror which, when held up to our own teaching, may show us some ways in which we can become more effective and creative educators. Like a good counselor or spiritual director, it will hopefully reflect elements of your own teaching experience back to you and offer you the opportunity to see it with new eyes. It is also intended to function like a diagnostician, guiding self-evaluation and self-diagnosis of our own pedagogies as we eavesdrop on conversations between neuroscientists and educators about the structure of our brains, how our brains learn, and how they create memory. It is not intended to be prescriptive of any particular method of teaching, but is designed primarily to be applied to face-to-face classroom situations, or, with some thought, possibly adapted to virtual classroom situations. It is not my intention to condemn current pedagogical practices in any classroom but, rather, to raise some questions and provoke you to ask additional questions about why you teach and how you teach.

The imaginary journey Dorothy Gale took to the Emerald City in the Land of Oz is a familiar archetypal journey of disorientation-orientation-reorientation and very similar to the journey on which we will embark: a journey to the Land of Sticky Learning. It doesn't take a brain surgeon to realize that the landscape of higher education has shifted, the classroom is not the same, and students are changing in a variety of ways, as noted above. We are clearly not in Kansas anymore! We need a variety of tools to help orient us for this journey, so we will equip ourselves by looking at various definitions and understandings of the nature of learning. In addition, we also need to understand how our brains work, so we will do a brief tour through some rudimentary neuroscience. Finally, we must understand the way in which memory is created, the different types of memory, and factors that influence the development of long-term memory. Once we have a basic understanding of the neurobiology, we can begin to reorient ourselves to new ways of teaching

4. Yonat Shimron, "Seminaries continue to attract older students," *Insights Into Religion*, http://religion insights.org/articles/seminaries-continue-attract-older-students.

5. Robin Steinke, interview with Fortress Press, Minneapolis, MN, February 25, 2013.

6. QR code URL: http://seminariumblog.org/?s=Nimble+Ways.

and learning through specific tips for sticky learning and reimagining the role of the instructor in a sticky learning environment.

Dorothy had companions on her journey to Oz: the Scarecrow, the Cowardly Lion, and the Tin Man. Our companions will come from diverse arenas, such as marketing and business, neuroscience and biology, psychology, education, and religion. The intersection of neuroscience with cognitive psychology in the late 1970s produced the field of cognitive neuroscience. Research since that time has examined how the structures of the brain work in areas of perception, action and behavior, learning and memory, language, and selective attention. Scientists have worked to discover how information and experience is received, retained, and retrieved in the brain. Educators and cognitive psychologists have begun to suggest ways in which cognitive neuroscience might inform educational theory and practice. Educators have become conversation partners with neurobiologists in order to understand better how their students learn and remember information and experiences. Across the country and at all levels of education, teachers and administrators are learning new ways to teach that optimize the conditions for long-term change to occur in a learner's brain.

While this book offers general principles for sticky learning and some illustrations of their application, the primary work of interpretation is left to you. Watch for opportunities to "MAKE IT STICK" throughout the book, sections that offer pauses for reflective questions or to engage with new concepts and ideas. Take time to wrestle with these concepts or assess the relevance of ideas or models for your class, your discipline, or your academic institution. Better yet, read this with a colleague from a different discipline and discuss it; question one another and push each other to wrestle with what sticky learning means in your context. This book will likely raise more questions than it answers but, hopefully, it will lead you to discover that the new territory of sticky learning is not so scary after all.

Part Two

Where We Are Headed

What would you do with a brain if you had one?
—Dorothy to the Scarecrow, *The Wizard of* Oz

Chapter 2

The Nature of Learning

Holly J. Inglis

What Does It Mean to Learn?

How does learning happen and, more importantly, how do you, as the teacher, know when learning is occurring? There are many different ways to understand the nature of learning, but this chapter will examine a cognitive way to understand and approach the nature of learning.

Cognition is simply the process of how we know what we know. The field of cognitive psychology, which examines processes such as attention, memory, problem solving, and creativity, has become an important conversation partner to education, helping educators to understand learning as processes in the brain that identify how knowing and remembering occur. The process of observing, categorizing, and connecting new information with what we already know comprises the basic way learning is defined in this view. The true learning occurs not because of the external information, or stimuli, but because of the inner cognitive work that is provoked by the developmental need of the learner to integrate information and make meaning and order out of their world.

Cognitive definition of learning: the process of observing, categorizing, and connecting new information with what we already know.

---

*QR code URL: http://seminariumblog.org/books/what-is-learning/.

Learning becomes a developmental task with identifiable markers at various stages of cognitive growth, with a goal of cumulative knowledge. Teaching depends on understanding the needs of learners at various ages and stages and providing sufficient information to stimulate the cognitive development without overloading the system. Psychologists such as Jean Piaget, Jerome Bruner, Lev Vygotsky, Benjamin Bloom, Howard Gardner, and others have been instrumental in laying the groundwork for understanding learning as a cognitive process, in affecting educational reforms, and ultimately reshaping educational theory and practice.

Piaget identified four stages of development in children: (1) sensory-motor, (2) intuitive/preoperational, (3) concrete operational, and (4) formal operational. Each stage was associated with a corresponding cognitive task. In the sensory-motor stage, a child understands her world through the five senses. During the intuitive/preoperational stage, a child develops the capacity for imagination and symbolic thought. In the concrete operational stage, a child can begin to use reason and logic to problem-solve, but only about things that are concrete and tangible. In the formal operational stage, we finally see a child who is able to think abstractly and symbolically, capable of deductive thinking, and creating and exploring hypotheses. More importantly, it is in this stage that we see the development of metacognition, or the ability to think about thinking. While Piaget did not focus his work on learning per se, his work informed others who adapted his theory in order to suggest educational reforms that more closely align with development. In addition, his work was groundbreaking in his assertion that children do not begin as a blank slate, but instead have a basic mental framework upon which all learning is built.

Design elements throughout the book called MAKE IT STICK invite you to integrate new information into your existing pedagogy.

Make It Stick

Since most of the developmental theorists focused their research on children, we need to consider how each of these theories might be compressed or appropriated into an adult-education learning environment. In a world-religions class, for example, you might choose to highlight the festivals celebrated by each religion. What are the senses engaged by the various festivals? Are there aspects of these festivals that can be enacted? What can be induced about those festivals by viewing videos of rituals? Move more concretely into the study of primary texts relating to the festivals. Finally, invite dialogue with adherents so as to begin to delve into the deeper significance of each festival. Consider the movement from senses to imagination to concrete problem solving to deductive thinking and metacognition as progressively more complex expressions of a particular theme.

Jerome Bruner is another cognitive psychologist, whose theories are frequently contrasted with those of Piaget. He views the learner as an active part of learning who is continually rebuilding his or her brain and mental/cognitive processes as information is received. Bruner has three stages of development: *enactive* (learning by doing), *iconic* (learning through pictures), and *symbolic* (learning through words). Learners—again, primarily children—in Bruner's work are innately curious and, when presented with a problem and evidence, will work to reconcile the information and discover a solution. This is known as discovery learning and gives rise to the notion of the teacher as a guide rather than a lecturer. Learning, for Bruner, is more than simply solving a problem that a teacher proposes. Learning as a cognitive process is natural, but is highly influenced by the richness of the environment that surrounds the learner and the degree to which learners are engaged in their environment. A stark learning environment will not stimulate development. The purpose of intentional instruction is to create this rich, engaging environment so that the naturally curious learner can make independent discoveries and construct new knowledge. Educators are not gatekeepers of knowledge, determining what learners will and will not learn, but are more like artists, creating a fertile environment and supporting the students' intellectual discoveries. The discovery-learning philosophy still influences education today in expeditionary schools across the country. Expeditionary schools are characterized by interdisciplinary study. Topics are usually explored in groups, and frequently this exploration occurs outside the classroom in the context of the community. Common forms of assessment include public presentations, compiled portfolios, and cumulative projects. What might an expeditionary religious-studies or seminary classroom look like?

To explore the philosophy of expeditionary schools, go here.

Make It Stick

While Bruner's theory also relates to the development of children's thinking, it could also be applied to adults learning new and unfamiliar material. For example, when adults encounter difficulties with learning at the symbolic stage, they sometimes revert to the earlier enactive or iconic stages in order to solve a problem. There is an undeniable element of play to Bruner's theory as well that undergirds the innovation of discovery. Certain subjects, such as cultural studies in religion and practical-theology courses in particular, may lend themselves more easily to learning by doing. How can you move from learning by doing to learning through pictures and then conclude by learning through words? In a course on "Religion in American Culture," for example, students will likely come with some knowledge of the role religion plays in our culture, whether positive or negative. Building on their existing knowledge, have students watch television and online media for references to religion (doing); assign either a culturally relevant contemporary movie with religious themes or a virtual visit to a contemporary art museum (pictures); pose an integrative activity that incorporates their observations and allows them to hypothesize about the meaning of their experiences, accompanied by a lecture that deepens their understanding (words).

Learning Happens Best through Interaction

Even though his primary research was also focused on children, the work of Lev Vygotsky is also equally applicable to adult learners. Like Bruner, Vygotsky believed that learning occurs independently through a natural curiosity, exploration, and imagination, but with a twist. His sociocultural research on cognitive development led him to propose that learning happens best when a child is "interacting with people in his environment and in cooperation with his peers."[1] In other words, the people in the learning environment become part of the curriculum. Whether these other individuals are part of the explicit curriculum—that is, explicitly stated outcomes or objectives that expect learners to interact with other learners and instructors collaboratively—or the implicit curriculum—that is, the invisible aspects of the organization, such as the organization of the class or the attitudes of instructors—will be determined by the philosophy of the learning institution or the professor herself. Unfortunately, in many circumstances and at all levels of education, the people in the learning environment are part of the null curriculum—that which is intentionally not taught. Students are not taught the value of collaboration and how to maximize the influence of others in the classroom for the benefit of the individual, primarily because the instructor may not understand this approach, may not accept its validity, or because it undermines the system of competition upon which most student success is defined.

Vygotsky's notion of cognitive learning is rooted in social interactions, but it is really about the development of independent problem-solving abilities and individual changes in behavior based on acquired information about our environment. He uses the term "Zone of Proximal Development," or ZDP, to define what happens in the context of social interaction. Take, for example, a student in a classroom who is presented with a problem he or she cannot solve independently. The educator invites students to work together to solve the problem, and intentionally pairs students who seem to have difficulty understanding the problem with those who are already beginning to problem-solve. Vygotsky claims that the distance between the abilities the individual child displays when working on his own and those the child develops with the social support of peers is the ZPD. He asserts that our natural drive for learning creates the ZPD, and therefore learning and development are best viewed as a social and collaborative activity. While Vygotsky's work focused on the

---

1. L. S. Vygotsky, *Mind in Society: The Development of Higher Psychological Processes*, ed. Michael Cole, Vera John-Steiner, Sylvia Scribner, and Ellen Souberman (Cambridge: Harvard University Press, 1978), 90.

cognitive development of children, his concepts are not only intriguing but stimulate us to think more deeply about the structure and setting of religious education for adults. For example, his notion that learning presupposes we possess an innate social nature and that we grow toward the intellectual life of those around us at key developmental moments leads me to reflect on the formal and informal ways in which students interact with other students, with instructors, with those outside the seminary and those in ministry contexts.[2] How, when, and even *if* we structure interactions among learners matters to learning, according to Vygotsky.

He suggests that pedagogy should look forward rather than backward.[3] He understands good learning—or, I would suggest, curiosity—to be in advance of development. Good learning pushes the learner into the unknown, the uncomfortable, and thereby requires him or her to lean more on other learners who are further along in their development, which of necessity pulls the less-developed learner up to a new level of knowing. For Vygotsky, learning beckons us forward and upward, fanning the flames of what we *do* know and enticing us toward what we *do not yet* know. What are your students curious about? If their curiosity drives their learning, how can you first identify, then utilize, their curiosity to fan the flames of their education?

When applied to classrooms, Vygotsky's principles suggest that social learning interactions should not be based primarily in the transmission of information and that the interactions that occur between learners, both within and beyond the classroom, are vital elements of learning. In fact, Vygotsky's principles might suggest that the conversations that occur after the conclusion of class, or in the coffee shop, or through the use of technology to continue and enhance the connection and interaction of the learners, not only expand the learning, but regenerate and prolong the learning, allowing learners to construct new understanding and knowledge for themselves. In my own seminary education, some of my most significant learning happened in the cafeteria. The cafeteria was where we all gathered after chapel, drawn in by the aroma of freshly baked cookies and newly brewed coffee, timed to coincide with the "Amen." That was where we asked the questions of one another that we could not or would not ask in class. That was where we wrestled with ideas and boldly challenged the notions of professors with whom we would not dare publically disagree in class. I would often leave with more questions than answers, but usually the sense of community and mutuality left me with a positive feeling. Enhanced by the delicious cookies, the cafeteria experience became a positive experience of learning for me.

Learning does not stop when the individual leaves the social context. Vygotsky takes us one step further by suggesting that the learning that takes place in a social, interactive context changes into learning that "sticks" with the individual. While higher levels of thinking and cognition originate as interactions between human beings (for Vygotsky, that means a child assisted or guided by an adult or a more-developed child), eventually the same processes, he claims, appear inside the individual without the influence of others.[4] In other words, social interactions may

2. Ibid., 88.

3. L. S. Vygotsky, *The Collected Works of L. S. Vygotsky*, vol. 2: *77 Fundamentals of Defectology*, ed. Robert W. Rieber and Aaron S. Carton, trans. Jane Knox and Carol B. Stevens (New York: Plenum, 1993), 251–52.

4. Vygotsky, *Mind in Society*, 57.

provoke the development of learning, but we are wired to make that learning our own at some point. Isn't this exactly what we want to occur in our students—learning that becomes "owned" and continues long after graduation and long after they assume their places in pulpits, or classrooms, or other vocational paths? As we will see later in our discussion on the development of memory, there are some factors that neuroscientists have identified which may make this process more effective.

One more piece from Vygotsky: the role of language. Many cognitive theorists, but Vygotsky in particular, emphasize the role of language as a primary form of interaction by which children learn from adults and adults transmit the vast body of knowledge that exists in our culture. Initially, the child receives the language from the adult, and eventually the child develops his or her own language in which to interpret the culture and direct their behavior. At first, this knowledge and thought is external to the children, but eventually it becomes internalized and becomes the child's own language. Granted, we are not dealing with children in a seminary or religious education classroom, but we are, in many ways, sharing a new language: the language of theological reflection. As we share this language with learners, we expect them to appropriate the language and use it to interpret or, in our language, exegete, the culture as well as our sacred texts. Do we have a similar expectation that they will internalize the language and make it their own?

Make It Stick

Vygotsky's theory has broad implications for the process of education that is based in the student's culture and may be particularly applicable to distance learning and nontraditional class schedules for working adults. Since learning must be applied directly into the students' culture in order to stick, look for opportunities to allow learning tasks to be relevant and action oriented. Given general learning goals, encourage your students to develop individual learning objectives that relate the content to their culture. Katherine Turpin, associate professor of religious education at Iliff School of Theology, Denver, has discovered how Vygotsky's approach can affect learning. Turpin teaches introductory religious education in a setting designed primarily for nontraditional students employed in religious institutions. She noticed the students seemed to be confused and unengaged with the content presented and decided to take a risk. Instead of beginning with the content, Turpin began with the experiences of the students and used their experiences and questions generated out of their experiences to guide the curriculum and, as a result, the students rated this particular class as highly relevant and effective.[5] Peer learning groups are applicable across many disciplines. Pose a problem related to the topic of study, such as determining criteria for what texts should be allowed in the canon, and then allow groups to wrestle to solve the problem. Content is presented by the instructor as groups raise questions in the problem-solving process.

---

5. Katherine Turpin, interview with author, Denver, CO, April 9, 2014.

An overview of constructivism and its influence on teaching and learning by Israel Galindo, Dean of Lifelong Learning at Columbia Theological Seminary.[6]

Moving from Teaching to Learning

Bruner and Vygotsky are among a group of cognitive psychologists who have been associated with a view of education known as *constructivism*. A constructivist view suggests that learning is a dynamic activity and occurs in the intersection of new information with the learner's prior knowledge. Knowledge is "constructed;" it is not delivered, or imparted, or imprinted. Constructivists believe that the reshaping of knowledge occurs best in the context of social interaction with other learners. Some would say that this requires a shift in focus in most school settings from "teaching" to "learning."

This model looks a great deal like Parker Palmer's notion of the educator as a leading learner, leading learners to new places where perhaps even the educator has never been.[7] The professor is no longer the focal point of the class and becomes a co-learner with the participants. In addition to being a co-learner, the leader must possess skills akin to those of a spiritual director, as well as biblical, theological, historical, or linguistic skills, or in some other particular area of knowledge. These skills are crucial to guide the learners in critically reflecting on their experiences and exegeting themselves and their experiences, both inside and outside the classroom. The exploration of the subject, or the "great thing," as Palmer calls it, drives the classroom in this model, rather than the content being predetermined by the instructor. That is not to say that a professor should not or does not prepare material, present information, or require activities from the students.

Indeed, Palmer's classroom looks very Vygotskian. Group projects are assigned in order to build consensus in learning within the group. Competition is avoided in favor of consensus in assessment as well. When the teacher holds the power of evaluation, then learning is skewed. We learn that what we believe will enable us to access some of the power. When evaluation and assessment are oriented away from judgment and more toward providing guidance for learning or course correction in the way in which a learner is approaching a problem, then, Palmer believes, learning is more effective.

> Teachers can give students a chance to have their work evaluated several times before it must be finished. Grading then becomes more a tool of learning and growth than a final judgment on the final product. But the largest leap a teacher can take beyond competition and toward consensus is to stop attaching grades exclusively to individuals and start

6. QR code URL: http://columbiaconnections.org/2014/06/20/what-is-constructivism/
7. Parker Palmer, *The Courage to Teach* (San Francisco: Jossey-Bass, 1998), 116.

assigning group tasks for which every member receives the same grade. When the academic reward system is used to make students rely on each other, the skills of consensus are more likely to be learned.[8]

The idea of a paradigm shift from "teaching" to "learning" has gained momentum in higher education in the past two decades. An article by Robert Barr and John Tagg in 1995 suggested that institutions of higher education were beginning to shift away from identifying themselves as institutions that exist to provide instruction, and moving toward viewing themselves and acting as institutions that produce learning.[9] Institutions are seeking to understand more about the nature of learning, which is born out of recent neuroscientific research on how our brains learn and on understanding the structure of the brain itself. This shift from a teaching approach to a focus on learning may be radically different from the model of schooling in which you participated and requires some corresponding significant shifts in understanding your role as teacher and the role of the learner. We wrestle with what it means to view learning as the active work of the student and the teacher as the leading learner, not passive or inactive, but no longer the sole source of information. It disrupts standard methods of content delivery, such as lecturing or a continuous, one-way stream of instruction and suggests that mastery of content may no longer be an effective end or purpose of learning. Chapter 5, below, will suggest some paradigm shifts that will promote a learning-centered model of education applicable to seminaries and religious studies.

Benjamin Bloom's taxonomy, first developed in the mid-1950s, although not by Bloom himself, is still used by educators to create scaffolded learning objectives. It has been updated to reflect newer models of understanding cognitive intellectual development and new educational tools, such as Web 2.0. By its very nature, the language of taxonomy moves from lower- to higher-order thinking, with remembering as the lowest level of thinking. This linear, hierarchical view of development is in sharp contrast to the truly web-like way in which the brain receives, processes information, and ultimately learns.

See this interactive model of Bloom's taxonomy revised.[10]

Bloom's taxonomy considers remembering, recall, and memory as a beginning stage of learning, which leads to higher levels, such as application and, eventually,

8. Parker Palmer, "Good Teaching: A Matter of Living the Mystery," Center for Courage & Renewal, http://www.couragerenewal.org/parker/writings/good-teaching/.
9. Robert B. Barr and John Tagg, "From Teaching to Learning—A New Paradigm for Undergraduate Education," *Change* (November/December 1995): 13–25.
10. QR code URL: http://www.celt.iastate.edu/teaching/RevisedBlooms1.html?utm_source=rss&utm _medium=rss&utm_campaign=a-model-of-learning-objectives.

creating. Some educators who are utilizing the work of cognitive psychology and neuroscience in learning and memory believe that retrieval of memories is the primary evidence of learning.[11] By this, they do not mean merely the retrieval of facts or details that have been crammed into our brains. Instead, they are referring to a process that pulls information from a variety of locations in the brain, combines and recombines it with new information, which results in a new product, new insight, a new method of problem solving. That is what is meant by creativity, and is the highest form of cognitive process in Bloom's taxonomy. Metacognition or teaching a student how to become an effective and autonomous learner for life is learning at a cosmic scale and requires an ability not only to know particular information but to be able to reflect on one's knowing. In a blog for Seminarium, Jane Webster talks about developing her own pedagogy of metacognition and offers some practical steps to begin to teach your students how to learn for life, which are well worth considering.

 Check out Dr. Jane Webster's Seminarium blog on teaching students how to learn for life.[12]

Make It Stick

Online learning is a particularly challenging pedagogical context, but Rob Kelly describes six ways to support an adult online learner that incorporates scaffolding techniques and guides them to greater awareness of their own learning.[13] In your online pedagogy, how do you invite students to recall previous learning experiences or knowledge? Do you encourage students to share not only insights but also struggles that arise out of a learning activity with one another, and support critical reflection that expresses knowledge they need to gain? Kelly points out that, particularly in online learning, structured feedback is very important and allows learners to accurately assess and self-regulate their learning. How predictable is your online class structure, how often do you monitor student engagement, and how frequently do you provide input or comment?

The Multiple Intelligences Theory of Howard Gardner is yet another cognitive view of how learning occurs. Gardner's work, like the other cognitive psychologists, was grounded in brain theory, but his theory of learning arose out of his study of people who had some form of brain injury or whose brains worked differently,

---

11. Marilee Sprenger, *Learning and Memory: The Brain in Action* (Alexandria, VA: Association for Supervision and Curriculum Development, 1999), 81.

12. QR code URL: http://seminariumblog.org/general/semclass/metacognition-teach-learn/.

13. Rob Kelly, "Six Ways to Support Adult Online Learners," *Faculty Focus*, http://www.facultyfocus.com/articles/online-education/six-ways-to-support-adult-online-learners/.

such as individuals with autism. When he observed that not all of an individual's abilities were gone even with a brain injury, it led him to suggest that intelligence is not monolithic; that we have more than one intelligence. In fact, he eventually suggested that we have nine different intelligences, or ways of knowing, and that while we all have all nine, we are inclined toward and work both intentionally and unintentionally to hone particular intelligences.

 See the nine intelligences of the "Multiple Intelligences Theory."[14]

Gardner's theory flew in the face of much of the accepted theory and practice of education when his work first appeared in the early 1980s. Still, it was a widely accepted theory and has driven a great deal of educational theory and practice with the assumption that teachers who become aware of the differing ways in which students best receive information, and then vary their teaching style to as many of the different ways as possible, increase the likelihood that their students will be able to learn and remember the information, and utilize the information to problem-solve.

Make It Stick

Take a few moments to review Gardner's nine intelligences. If you are not familiar with the intelligences, see the QR code or the related URL above. What were the primary intelligences that were used in your own educational experiences, particularly in your advanced academic instruction? What are the primary intelligences used in your own classroom instruction? What are the most comfortable pedagogical methods to which you frequently return and how do they correlate with Gardner's intelligences?

If your answer to the questions in the "MAKE IT STICK" section is verbal/linguistic and mathematical/logical intelligences, you are not alone. Multiple Intelligences Theory has been the guiding principle for how we think about our students and structure our learning environments for over two decades, both in the seminary and religious-studies classroom and in ministry settings. I learned about MI (Multiple Intelligences) Theory in a "Christian Education Theory" classroom and believed that if I created learning environments that utilized as many of the modes as possible to transmit information, then I was being an effective educator and that my students would be engaged, would automatically connect with the information, and thereby would retain and apply the information. In reality, once I got into parish ministry, I knew that was not consistently occuring, but I had no better way to define learning, and, in fact, had no good way of assessing learning

---

14. QR code URL: http://web.cortland.edu/andersmd/learning/MI%20Table.htm.

effectively except to evaluate the number of intelligences that were used during a particular class. Academic classrooms are not the same as a church classroom, to be sure, but the challenge to understand, foster, and assess learning is similar. Gardner understood intelligence as multidimensional. Learning is also multidimensional; cognitive learning theory and neuroscience tell us that there is no one way to understand learning. Welcome to the postmodern world of education!

Despite the ways Multiple Intelligences Theory has become ingrained in our pedagogical thinking, Howard Gardner himself stated at a lecture at the "Learning and the Brain" conference in 2011 that he moved beyond the theory a decade ago and that educators should also move on. Gardner suggested that, rather than focusing on intelligences, educators also should understand the concept of the different minds within an individual. You can easily see the correlation between the intent of theological and religious-studies education and Gardner's five minds: the disciplined mind, the synthesizing mind, the creating mind, the respectful mind, and the ethical mind.[15] Gardner begins his discussion of the disciplined mind by describing research based on a classroom scenario in which a student has been instructed in a concept or theory and has repeatedly solved problems directly correlated to the learned theory. However, when asked to solve a problem that is based on the learned theory but is not identical to the previously solved problem, or which is unfamiliar to the student, the student cannot. In fact, the research indicates that many of the students who have been schooled in the concept or theory will give the same answers to the new problem as students who have not taken the course and received the instruction. You can understand how this would be most discouraging to a professor. What's going on here? Gardner says that, while these students have genuinely learned lots of facts and knowledge about a particular subject, they have not learned to think in a disciplined or synthesized manner—that is, to understand the reasons behind the concepts or theories or knowledge gained and to be able to appropriate them in new settings or applications that consolidate the information into new behavior or responses in each new situation. Reading this book will not necessarily lead to disciplined or synthesized learning. However, processing the information and practices either alone or with peers, using the MAKE IT STICK conventions and your own reflections, can lead to synthesis and creative pedagogy.

Gardner is not the only one to note this phenomenon. Professor Eric Mazur of Harvard, who coincidentally advocates a shift from "teaching" to "helping students learn,"[16] was disturbed by an article by David Hestenes that he read in the *American Journal of Physics*. Hestenes reported results from a specially devised test to evaluate students' understanding of physics after an introductory course that focused primarily on rote memorization of formulas and basic information about physics. While the students could perform the functions of basic physics, Hestenes found that they held the same misconceptions after the course as they did prior to the course and lacked ability to connect the laws of physics with the real world. Mazur decided to try out the test on his own students and was dismayed to find similar

15. Howard Gardner, *Five Minds for the Future* (Boston: Harvard Business Press, 2008), 3.
16. Craig Lambert, "Twilight of the Lecture," *Harvard Magazine* (March-April 2012), http://harvard magazine.com/2012/03/twilight-of-the-lecture.

results. The students could solve problems by rote by applying the formulas that they had memorized but failed to demonstrate "a real world understanding of the concepts behind the problems."

Give a Fish or Teach to Fish?

What are Gardner, Mazur, and Hestenes telling us about our own teaching and our own classrooms? Gardner is concerned that we are teaching subject matter rather than how to think about the subject matter. Students are consumed with mastering the subject matter rather than learning how to manipulate the subject matter. We certainly want our students to develop ways of thinking theologically and critically about the world, but how does that goal balance with the extent to which we still expect them to commit facts, dates, names to memory? To be sure, detailed information is important and vital in many academic disciplines, but if a discipline is a distinctive way of thinking about the world, how do we envision our students using those things that they commit to memory in a disciplined way once they leave the classroom and encounter unfamiliar problems or situations? Mazur and Hestenes are spurring us to examine our pedagogy in light of interactive peer learning, in much the same way as Vygotsky first theorized. Maybe you'd like to replicate their research in your classroom to see if your students are developing disciplined minds or are preoccupied with mastering the subject matter. What will you change if your research aligns with Mazur and Hestenes?

Cognitive-learning skills, which many educators assert are vital to the development of long-term memory and effective integration of new information as it is received by the brain, are part of the larger umbrella of cognition, or the ability to process information, think and reflect on the information, articulate thoughts and reflections, and relate it to what is already known. For adult learners in a seminary or religious-studies context, a constructivist view of learning based in cognitive psychology suggests that learning is a continuous process of modifying what they already know, blending experience, understanding, and knowledge with thoughts and feelings. The result is a wise learner.

As we draw our exploration of learning to a close, here are some key points to carry with us as we turn to explore the physiological structure of the brain and how it learns:

- Learning is about actively creating meaning and order out of our experiences as learners see, do, and connect.
- Prior knowledge or understanding about a particular subject exerts an influence on learning.
- The goal of the teacher is to provoke a cognitive change in the way the learner processes his or her world and in the way in which they view themselves, others, and the world.
- Learning is the active work of the student and the teacher functions as the leading learner, not passive or inactive, but engaged as a co-learner.
- Learning cooperatively provides opportunity for stimulating higher-level thinking skills and is an important source of motivation.

Chapter 3

How the Brain Works

Holly J. Inglis

Hopefully, your mind (read brain) has been changed, or altered, by the fact that you have been reading this book and thinking about your students and yourself. The assertion that learning is change is more than a claim by cognitive psychologists. It is, in reality, a physical fact of the brain. As we learn, our brain changes.

The brain has traditionally been identified in three basic parts: the *reptilian* brain, the *mammalian* brain, and the *human* brain. Of course, the brain is a highly complex system and, therefore, our discussion of the brain here will be simple, providing us with basic understanding of its structures, the way it works, and how learning takes place in the brain. We will need some brain vocabulary in order to be conversant. Here are few of the most important terms:

Lobes: There are four outer lobes of the brain, each of which has an area called an association cortex, which holds information temporarily until it is either dumped, forgotten, or sent on to memory. Think of the cortex as the first responder to incoming stimuli of each type.

Frontal lobe—contains the primary motor cortex
Parietal lobe—contains the primary sensory cortex
Occipital lobe—contains the primary visual cortex
Temporal lobe—contains the primary auditory cortex

The cerebellum, at the base of the brain, is associated with regulation and coordination of movement, posture, and balance and, as we will see later, is important as a memory storehouse.

---

*QR code URL: http://www.youtube.com/watch?v=AyZi-YaE4Vc. This video, called "The Brain Show," condenses basic brain structure during its seventeen minutes.

Deep inside the brain lies the fifth lobe known as the *limbic system*. There are two important players in this system that help the brain process information and develop memory: the *hippocampus* and the *amygdala*. The hippocampus functions much like a university library that is a vast repository for knowledge: it catalogs and files the factual information that the brain receives and learns, storing both trivial and important information. In order to do well at trivia games, you are accessing

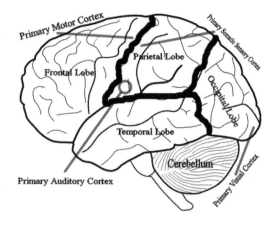

your hippocampus. It does not house all your memories, but it catalogs them and sends them for permanent placement in other long-term memory storage units in the brain. In an issue of *National Geographic* magazine focusing on memory, science journalist Joshua Foer says that while our memories are not actually stored in the hippocampus, it is the part of the brain that makes them stick.[1]

The amygdala resides next to the hippocampus. It is the relay station for emotional information, screening incoming information and determining if it is emotionally important for long-term storage. This very sensitive brain part is relevant in every information transmission. Think of someone you have met recently—a friend, colleague, student, someone at your faith community, or someone from a completely different setting, such as a child's athletic team or a business connection. Where did you encounter them? Was it in a regular context in which you usually encounter them or was it out of context? Did you have any difficulty remembering their name? What was your reaction to them? Were you at ease, or were you anxious or defensive, or did you have any other emotional response? In your encounter with this person you accessed both your hippocampus and your amygdala, and here is how you can remember these two important parts of

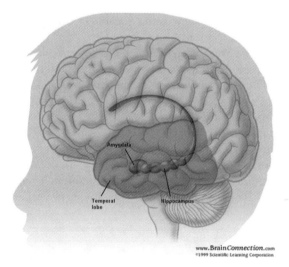

www.Brain*Connection*.com
©1999 Scientific Learning Corporation

---

1. Joshua Foer, "Remember This," *National Geographic* (November 2007), 36.

our brains. The hippocampus tells you who someone is; it recalls factual information. The amygdala tells you how you feel about that person; it recalls emotional information.

Before we get to exactly how learning occurs in the brain, we need to understand how the brain receives information to send to the appropriate lobe and/or cortices. The simple explanation of an extremely complex neurological and biological process is this: we take information into our brains through our five senses. What we hear, and a small part of what we taste, touch, and see is filtered through the brain stem, then goes to the thalamus. The thalamus is located in the middle of the central core of the brain, wrapped in the arms of the hippocampus. It plays a significant role acting as a busy relay station for many sensory and motor signals. It also acts as a center for detecting pain and is involved in sleep.

You will notice I did not mention smell in relation to the thalamus. Smell is tricky. There is a nerve, called the olfactory nerve, which goes directly into the amygdala and olfactory cortex without going through the thalamus. Think about the last time you entered a setting where food had been cooking. Almost before you can take a breath to inhale the smells, your olfactory nerve has shot the information into your amygdala and you have a neuro-emotional response to the smell. Usually, it's something like, "What smells so good?," but smells can trigger emotional memories that recall times, places, and people which are all associated with that smell. Your brain processes smell much quicker and more definitively than your other senses. Why? Think about where your nose is located—right above your mouth. What's the first thing you do when you take something out of the fridge that's been in there a bit too long? You smell it in order to know whether it is safe to eat. Next time you do that and you get a quick "no thanks" back from your brain, thank your olfactory nerve.

Communicate, Communicate, Communicate

Now that we have taken a quick tour of the brain, we are ready to see how learning happens in the brain. Remember that the reason we learn is to make meaning and order out of our experiences, and so all the activity of the brain is purposed to this end. Learning occurs in the brain when two neurons communicate.[2] A neuron is an electrically excitable cell that processes and transmits information by electrochemical signals via connections with other cells.

Learning occurs in the brain when neurons communicate.

Your hand and your forearm are convenient representations of a neuron. If you stretch out your hand in front of you with your palm up, the palm of your

---

2. Marilee Sprenger, *Learning and Memory: The Brain in Action* (Alexandria, VA: Association for Supervision and Curriculum Development, 1999), 2.

hand can be compared to the cell body of a neuron. Information enters the cell body through appendages called dendrites, represented by your fingers. Wiggle your fingers. Just as your fingers move, your dendrites are constantly moving as they seek information from other neurons. When a neuron has received information and needs to pass the information on to another neuron, the message is sent through the axon. When a neuron sends information down its axon to another neuron, it never actually touches the other neuron. The message has to go from the axon of the sending neuron to the dendrite of the receiving neuron by "swimming" through a space called the synapse. This is a vastly simplified presentation of the way neurons work, but the important thing to remember is that for learning to take place, neurons must make connections.

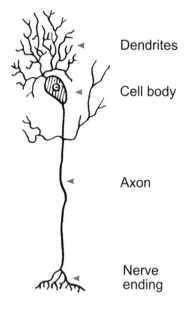

Dendrites

Cell body

Axon

Nerve ending

As the neurons make connections, the brain is growing dendrites and strengthening the synapses. Although different neurons fire at different speeds, researchers believe it is reasonable to estimate that a neuron can fire about once every five milliseconds, or about two hundred times a second. Most researchers estimate the human brain contains approximately one hundred billion neurons and between five hundred trillion and one quadrillion synapses. Here is a trivia question you can use at your next cocktail party: How many neurons can fit on the head of a pin? The answer is thirty thousand. Impressive, but wait! Each neuron may be linked with another five to ten thousand neurons. That's a lot of communicating going on in our heads and it means our brains are taking in lots of information, whether that information is coming in intentional ways or arriving from unintended sources.

In addition, there are different types of neurons that transmit different kinds of information. Sensory neurons transmit sensory information, such as touch, temperature, sight, and sound received from cells in the body. Interneurons function as relays of information between neurons. Motor neurons communicate information from the brain to muscles in the body, resulting in action or movement in response to stimuli. But how do the neurons transmit these various types of information to other neurons?

The transmission within a neuron is electrical and the transmission between neurons is chemical. The chemicals present in this electrical neuron dance are called neurotransmitters. These have familiar names like dopamine, serotonin, epinephrine (commonly called adrenaline) and norepinephrine, but there are many types; over sixty have been identified so far. The neurotransmitter is the chemical substance that enables the information to cross the synaptic gap, which some neuroscientists measure at .02 microns. Once these chemicals have been released by the brain cells and picked up by the neurons, they have a powerful influence on how

Table 3.1

Neurotransmitter	What it does
EXCITATORY NEUROTRANSMITTERS	
Epinephrine (adrenaline)	Stimulates body movement in fearful or dangerous situations; triggered by emotional responses
Norepinephrine	Gets your brain's attention; tells your brain to be alert, high levels can cause aggression; resides in the amygdala
INHIBITORY NEUROTRANSMITTERS	
Dopamine	Controls smooth physical movement; regulates flow of information into higher levels of the brain; correlated with attention, can have a euphoric effect; low levels can affect working memory
Serotonin	"Feel-good" neurotransmitter; aids in smooth transmission of messages in the brain and body; low serotonin can create depression or low self-esteem and a feeling of being trapped in emotions; regulates mood and sleep

we think, feel, and act. Table 3.1 identifies the primary effects of the most familiar of these complex and powerful chemicals on a student's brain and behavior.[3]

 If your brain needs more information about neurotransmitters, go to this site. (Don't be swayed by the title of the page; neurotransmitters aren't just for kids!)[4]

The brain may release these chemicals as the result of exercise, an affirming touch or smile, or a meaningful relationship. Research has indicated a positive release of "feel-good" chemicals when participants are part of a team. Other researchers are studying the positive effects of music in the release of neurotransmitters and suggest that listening to background music that makes you "feel good" prior to undertaking a task can actually increase your attention and memory. Why not experiment with this in your educational setting? Invite your learners to bring music that makes them "feel good" and take a few minutes at the start of class for them to listen individually on their personal devices, before beginning your tasks. See how they feel at the end of class. If they feel as if they learned more, perhaps you can break into the Hallelujah Chorus!

---

3. Ibid., 22–25.
4. QR code URL: https://faculty.washington.edu/chudler/chnt1.html.

On the converse side, neurotransmitters can be affected negatively by outside influences—such as the food we eat and the chemicals we consume, such as caffeine, alcohol, and other substances that alter the normal activity of our brain—sleep, mental health, exercise, and stress. While moderate stress pushes the brain to work harder, stress over a long period of time, or chronic stress, has been shown to decrease performance. Under stress of any kind, our brains simply do not perform as well. The production of stress hormones, like cortisol, inhibits the production of other neurotransmitters, like serotonin, which is associated with sleep. The more sleep is affected, the more the stress is felt, resulting in a vicious cycle, which affects our ability to pay attention and, more importantly, affects the entire process of learning. Brooke Lester's Seminarium blog highlights the impact of sleep deprivation in academia for both students and faculty.

 Scan this code for Brooke Lester's "Seminarium" blog—*Sleep in Academia* series.[5]

Artists of Learning/Masters of Teaching

The research of neuropsychiatrist and Nobel laureate Dr. Eric Kandel on sea slugs revealed that learning rewires the brain, resulting in the functional reorganization of the brain each time learning occurs.[6] Kandel, along with scientists in a variety of fields from biology to psychiatry, studies the nature of learning from a physiological and neurological perspective. From this approach, learning is about the constant remaking and reshaping of our neuronal structures, which is beyond the conscious control of the learner, but not beyond the ability of a teacher to affect. James Zull and John Medina are two influential scientists whose work is not only important to understanding the physiological nature of learning, but also to understanding the development of memory.

Learning is the constant remaking and reshaping of our neuronal structures due primarily to external stimuli.

James Zull is a professor of biology and director of the University Center for Innovation in Teaching and Education at Case Western Reserve University. His scholarship, based in decades of brain research, focuses on understanding how

5. QR code URL: http://seminariumblog.org/curator/sleep-in-academia-the-brain-weve-got/.
6. John Medina, *Brain Rules* (Seattle: Pear Press, 2008), 57.

brain research informs teaching. Once
again, Zull sounds a familiar refrain:
"Learning is change. It is change in
ourselves, because it is change in the
brain. Thus the art of teaching must
be the art of changing the brain."[7] In
his own study of how our brains comprehend, he happened upon a book
by David Kolb entitled *Experiential
Learning*, in which Kolb describes a
four-stage cycle that facilitates deep
learning. Simply stated, Kolb's cycle,
which relies on John Dewey and Jean
Piaget, looks like this:[8]

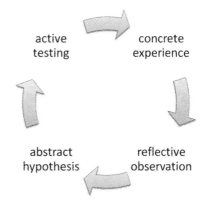

active testing — concrete experience — reflective observation — abstract hypothesis

Zull knew that Kolb was on to something. The cycle of learning Kolb described
was nearly identical to the biological cycle of the brain with which Zull was so
familiar. He integrated Kolb's work with his own, showing a link with the biological
way the brain works and aligning the four tasks of learning with the four cortices of
the brain.[9] It was a "natural" connection.

See Zull's image of the Learning Cycle.[10]

Zull believes it is impossible to separate teaching from learning. This may sound
opposite from the constructivists' call to shift toward learning rather than focus
on teaching, but I believe they both issue a call to educators to become artists of
learning rather than masters of teaching. Zull says the cycle primarily begins with
concrete, sensory experience, but does not always flow in one direction or start in
one place because the structure of the brain demonstrates that communication
between the various cortices goes in different directions and back and forth. The
point is that this model of how we learn matches how our brains are wired.

We know the brain changes when we learn, but what causes those changes, and
are those changes permanent? James Zull has two answers: practice and emotion.
John Medina has *twelve* answers, which he calls "Brain Rules."[11] As a molecular biol-
ogist, Medina makes understandable the complex world of neuroscience and how
the brain works. Each rule has implications for your classroom and your pedagogy.

---

7. James Zull, *The Art of Changing the Brain* (Sterling, VA: Stylus, 2002), xiv.
8. Ibid., 17.
9. Ibid., 18.
10. QR code URL: http://sharpbrains.com/blog/2006/10/12/an-ape-can-do-this-can-we-not/.
11. John Medina, "12 Brain Rules," in *Brain Rules*, http://www.brainrules.net/the-rules.

Three rules in particular enhance our discussion of how the brain works to create learning.

 To download a poster of Medina's Brain Rules, go to this link.[12]

Get 'Em Movin'

Exercise boosts the brain's ability to learn, as Medina notes in his Rule #1,[13] and as John Ratey, author of *Spark: The Revolutionary New Science of Exercise*, also explains. Researchers are not precisely certain how exercise affects learning, but certainly the physical results of exercise—increased blood flow and increased oxygen—provide an enriched environment for neurons and brain tissue. According to some neuroscientists, aerobic activity, such as walking, running, or other cardio exercise boosts the ability of the brain to focus, pay attention, and solve problems,[14] which is precisely how educators desire their students to participate in a class setting. Remember the neurotransmitters? Endorphins, also a neurotransmitter, are also involved in the connection between exercise and learning. They actually clobber the stress hormones and neurotransmitters in the brain as well. If you have ever felt really good after a run or a workout session, and then took a shower or grabbed a bite to eat, then you missed a prime opportunity to engage in new learning if you didn't run right home and break out a book or tackle some writing project.

Action and movement are an important beginning to the process of learning and, as we will discuss later, action completes the cycle of learning. Exercise and movement also support the development of memory associated with the learning. As a church educator, I can attest to the memorable learning that occurs on mission trips or at church camps, both of which revolve around and incorporate movement and exercise. Perhaps you have similar memories of events in your life, or perhaps your institution offers service days, where faculty and students go out into the community to engage in community service. It is not learning in a classroom, and it will not show up on any test, but it can be profound learning together.

Picture your classroom or learning space. Without extensive research, it is reasonable to suggest that most seminary classrooms are not equipped with treadmills or running tracks. Some barely have enough room to maneuver between the fixed tables, desks, and chairs. How long are your classes? In one seminary class I observed recently, class was scheduled for three hours twice a week. Normally, the professor gave a fifteen-minute break after the first hour and a half—time to allow

---

12. QR code URL: http://www.brainrules.net/the-rules.
13. Medina, *Brain Rules*, 8–28.
14. A. F. Kramer, et al., "Aging, fitness and neurocognitive function," *Nature* 400 (July 1999): 418–19.

the students to walk briskly across campus, get a cup of coffee, and return to the classroom. This is not the most effective use of movement to enhance learning, but is undoubtedly better than sitting for three hours consistently. How long have you been sitting while reading this book? If it has been longer than thirty minutes, you need to get up and move to a different location, do some stretches, or take a walk, but only if you want to remember what you have read and thought. But if you are reading this book while working out on a treadmill, there is a likelihood that your brain is firing at a faster pace than my brain as I sit passively in a chair writing this sentence. Do you incorporate movement into your learning experiences? Does your discipline lend itself easily to action or is it more difficult for you to imagine incorporating movement into your class in a relevant and creative manner?

To Stress or Not to Stress

We talked earlier about stress and its effect on learning. We all have it. Some people say stress is neither good nor bad; how you handle it is what makes the difference. But the presence of stress hormones and neurotransmitters like epinephrine do make a difference in how we learn. Medina's #3 Rule is that stressed brains learn differently.[15]

What were the stressors for you in your own education? Reflect on your students. What are the stressors in their lives and how are they similar or different to your own stresses? Elementary-school teachers know that the stresses faced by today's children dramatically affects their performance in the classroom. Our nation's children face economic hardships, substance abuse in their homes, violence in their homes and their neighborhoods, inability to sleep due to fears or noise or hunger. Today's adult students are not likely to face those kinds of stresses, but consider things like debt, job prospects, denominational examination processes, being away from family systems of support, working one or more jobs while taking classes, plus the invisible stresses that we may never see, such as relationship stresses, health stresses, mental-health issues. The stress we place upon students in an academic environment is by far not the only stress with which they must deal; they are affected by all the other stressors in their lives as well. When a student walks into your classroom, their stress walks in with them and affects their ability to learn, both positively and negatively.

During stress, our emotional brains are engaged. Remember the amygdala? Depending on the reaction to the stress, our emotions could actually be heightened and possibly create an emotionally charged learning experience that becomes part of our memory. And do not negate the hippocampus! Imagine a ham at Christmas covered with whole cloves and you have a picture of the hippocampus, covered in cortisol receptors, just waiting for the chemical to come its way and BANG! You're alert, watching, aware, just in case a threat is near. That same state of alertness can actually contribute to learning in some circumstances. Teachers who understand

---

15. Medina, *Brain Rules*, 169.

how to use stress effectively to create alertness can contribute to their students' learning.

Stress is one part of what makes our brain an "emotional brain." Earlier, we discussed the amygdala as part of the limbic system of the brain. In the 1990s, Joseph LeDoux,[16] a researcher at the State University of New York at Stony Brook, proposed that there may be no such thing as the limbic system and it is not a valid concept in and of itself for understanding emotion and motivation. His research on rats led him to suggest that there is a distinction between feelings and emotion. Simply stated, LeDoux says emotions are the immediate and rapid physiological responses to a stimulus. He gives the example of seeing a snake on a path while you are hiking. Feelings, on the other hand, take more time and use slower pathways in the brain. LeDoux says the frontal cortex is involved in the process of feelings and actually does a detailed analysis of the information, bringing in information from many parts of the brain to make an "informed" decision, which is then sent back to the amygdala, either affirming or quelling the initial response called for by the amygdala.[17] Once the situation has been assessed and your brain figures out that it is indeed a stick and not a snake, then the amygdala is informed to stand down; no running is necessary.

Regardless of whether we are talking about feelings or emotions, LeDoux's research sought to bridge the gap he perceived in cognitive neuroscience between cognition and emotion. The take-away from LeDoux's work is simply that (1) we do have emotional responses to stimuli and (2) the brain has a complex response to emotionally laden stimuli. Emotion is a part of how our brain works and can include a bodily response if the frontal cortex determines it is necessary. If teachers can gain a better understanding of the role emotion plays in the process of learning, they can potentially alter the emotional experience for students and create greater opportunity for learning to occur and memory to develop.

The emotional brain is a bit like a hornet's nest, however: once you've stirred it up, it's really hard to calm it down. You have no idea of the emotional baggage or history your students bring to the classroom, so your best efforts to stimulate an emotional response that is appropriate may trigger some other, greater emotional response than you anticipated. Without a doubt, teachers should not use emotion casually in the classroom nor attempt to manipulate students. Far from being manipulative, paying attention to the role of emotion in your classroom can become a powerful hook for new information, which we will learn more about in the next section.

What captures our emotion also captures our attention, and what we learn in that emotional experience does have sticking power for good or ill. Emotion and feeling are not always linked to the presentation of information or content, however. Sometimes, it is simply a response to the physical environment. If a learning environment is too cold, too hot, too close to the cafeteria so you get the smell of

16. Joseph E. LeDoux, "The Emotional Brain, Fear, and the Amygdala," *Cellular and Molecular Neurobiology* 23, nos. 4/5 (2003): 727–28.
17. Joseph E. LeDoux, "Emotion, Memory and the Brain," *Scientific American* 220 (June 1994): 50–57.

lunch wafting into your room, then your students may be focusing more on these factors than the factors in fifteenth-century society that fomented the Reformation.

When you intentionally create stress in the learning environment, you are asking your students to produce neurotransmitters that can enhance the experience and provoke new approaches to problem solving. The more intense the experience, the more adrenaline is emitted, and the stronger the likelihood that the experience and the learning that takes place during the experience will stick with the student—but be careful. Here is something to remember about stress in general: the more we feel out of control or that we have lost control, the greater the negative impact of the stress we are experiencing and the more we are likely to focus on survival instincts rather than learning something from the situation. Emotion is a two-edged sword and can easily detract from learning. Novelty, as well as emotion, will seize our attention; the emotion, however, must always serve the message.

Problem Seekers and Problem Solvers

Our tendency to be natural explorers, Medina's Rule #8,[18] is what makes us life-long learners and what drives the creative, problem-solving processes in our brains from the moment of our birth. It is the "brains," so to speak, behind collaborative learning. The right prefrontal cortex is instrumental in our exploration by looking for errors in our hypotheses or conclusions; if it discovers we have missed some important details, like the stick in the path that is indeed not a stick but is a snake and a potentially poisonous one, then another area of the cortex along with the hypothalamus sends a neural message to change our behavior and evacuate. This continuous process of taking in sensory observations, hypothesizing about our observations, testing our hypotheses, and arriving at conclusions mirrors Zull's Four Pillars of Learning.[19]

Our brains lead us to be problem seekers and problem solvers. How we gather the information matters, and the sensory observations can be intentional activities created by a teacher or unintentional events, such as the temperature of the classroom. The information can be visual, auditory, olifactory, or physical. Gathering or receiving the information, however, does not automatically lead to understanding, as Zull notes. "Learning is not equal to data collection."[20] Each form of sensory data is valuable and provides various kinds of stimulation for the brain. Visual data is quite powerful and trumps the other senses. Most of our sensory observations come through hearing. Smell and taste are, believe it or not, primarily emotional observations. If someone has had garlic or blue cheese for lunch and walks into the classroom, we are likely to observe that fairly quickly and have an immediate emotional and behavioral response.

What about the second- or third-career students in your classroom? Are they able to make sensory observations at the same rate as the younger students? While

---

18. Medina, *Brain Rules*, 261.
19. James E. Zull, "Key Aspects of How the Brain Learns," *New Directions for Adult and Continuing Education* 110 (Summer 2006): 5.
20. Ibid.

it is true, sadly, that we do lose some of our synaptic connections as we age (some researchers estimate as high as thirty thousand neurons per day),[21] it is also true that we continue to create neurons in the areas of our brain that have been identified as important to learning and, furthermore, these new neuronal pathways demonstrate the same characteristics for adaptation and change as those of an infant. My ninety-one-year-old father-in-law is a perfect example. Rather than sit idly watching TV or staring out a window, he spends his days napping and watching TED Talks on his computer, often calling to tell us about the newest thing he's learned. He continues to read and prefers nonfiction. He is a lifelong problem solver. He struggles to find others who share his love of continued learning and finds, sadly, that he is just a tad sharper than most of his living companions. Having graduated from Yale Seminary, I have no doubt that he will want to read this book . . . and then talk about it with me.

Squirrel!

Curiosity is a curious thing. It is the stuff of discovery and distraction. In order to understand what I am about to say you need to understand my context. I am writing this book while sitting at my desk at our mountain home. At seven-thousand-feet elevation, I am surrounded by evergreen-covered hills, azure blue skies, and sunrises to die for. At first glance, this would seem an idyllic spot in which to express my creativity. Quite the contrary! Outside my window, I saw two yellowtail hawks circling in the wind. I heard ruby-throated hummingbirds zip past, barely stopping to sip nectar from the feeder. I refocused myself, returned to my writing, and was rolling along well until my ears caught the sound of a bird I didn't recognize. I jumped up from my desk to discover a western tanager at my birdfeeder, which resulted in at least a fifteen-minute exploration in my bird book and online. I feel a bit like Dug, the talking dog, in the Pixar movie *Up!* who is easily distracted by squirrels. Clearly, I cannot bird watch and write a book at the same time!

There's no way around it. The brain simply cannot multitask, yet while I am constructing my thoughts, I am working on a computer with two screens and have three different programs open and seven Internet tabs open simultaneously, plus two books open in my lap. You may not be a tech-savvy teacher, but your students are certainly likely to be tech-savvy learners. In a seminary classroom, I observed over 90 percent of the students using electronic devices as a classroom tool, supported and encouraged by the instructor. What the instructor did not see was what was on the screens of those devices. The learning-management software (LMS) was open to the class notes for the day, but so was their email, Facebook, YouTube, and more. Oh yes, and their phones were on silent but sitting nearby in case a vital text message came in while the professor was lecturing. You know the scenario.

As part of Rule #8 on attention, John Medina says clearly that "multitasking, when it comes to paying attention, is a myth."[22] Over the past decade, research-

21. Medina, *Brain Rules*, 271.
22. Ibid., 84.

ers have delved into finding out exactly how our brains have changed, rewired, structurally shifted due to the influence of technology, but the fact still remains that when we attempt to perform two or more cognitive tasks at once, or pay attention to two or more things at the same time, the brain splits its focus among the frontal lobes. The more complex the tasks and the more the tasks need to be remembered, the more our brain works to prioritize one activity over the others. Research indicates that when two complex tasks are juggled, we exhibit something called "continuous partial attention," so that we are not fully able to grasp concepts, principles, and data. Like switching between two windows on your computer, there is a microsecond of lag time. The same process is true of your brain, which results in lowered effectiveness in both tasks. When researchers introduced a third task in a multitasking experiment, the brain became overwhelmed. In its attempt to prioritize the tasks, the brain chose one task to focus on, put one less-important task on the back burner, and completely forgot about one of the three tasks.[23] Did you know that heavy multitasking can temporarily lower our IQ by as much as fifteen points? While looking for a new job, my husband pointed out how many jobs, even in education and technology, include "ability to multitask" in the list of desired skills. If these employers only understood that by asking for someone who regularly multitasks, they are, in reality, asking for someone who works less effectively. We multitask not only because of time constraints, but because we think it makes us more productive. A study by Realization[SM], a project-management software company, showed that the effects of multitasking are tangible and dramatic not only for the individual, but also for the organization that employs individuals who are either asked to multitask or do so independently.[24] It actually decreases our productivity as well as increases the time required to complete the tasks, but more important for our consideration is the fact that when our brains try to juggle multiple cognitive tasks, it decreases our ability to comprehend information fully and to differentiate between relevant and irrelevant information. That can be a problem in an educational scenario!

One final word about the amazing brains of the students with whom we engage. Earlier we described the way the brains of older learners continue to grow new connections, even into our nineties. But what about younger students who are coming straight from undergraduate education? I am sure you could hypothesize, from your own sensory observations, that their brains are different, depending on their age and stage of life, as well as other circumstances. You may observe that younger students learn differently, but do you know why?

There are two things we need to know when discussing the brains of the twenty-something students. First, there is a new category of development that bridges the time between adolescence and adulthood called "emerging adulthood." Emerging adults are eighteen to twenty-nine years old. Many psychologists, sociologists, and neuroscientists see this as a distinct stage of life with distinct characteristics.

---

23. Nicklas Prieto, "Dubunking the Myth of Multitasking at the Office," Docstoc, http://www.docstoc.com/article/168729842/Debunking-the-Myth-of-Multitasking-at-the-Office.

24. Realization[SM], "The Effects of Multitasking on Organizations," http://www.realization.com/the-effects-of-multitasking-on-organizations.

Research on the adolescent brain indicates that the prefrontal lobe, responsible for executive functions, impulse control, and consequential thinking, may not be fully developed in adolescents. Many of us in higher education, however, as well as in the church and even in our own families, see characteristics of adolescent thinking and processing in some of the young adults with whom we work. Because we work in an environment where calling and vocation are part of our institutional and theological vocabulary, we may assume that our emerging adults have a grasp on their career trajectory. This may not be the case. Instead, you may find that some of them are exploring ministry or even exploring themselves and their faith. Some institutions have even developed a special academic track for just such a purpose. Researchers indicate there are also economic factors that contribute to this delayed adulthood and when we look at the employment futures for graduates of theological institutions, it's not always a bright picture, with denominations continuing to lose members, downsizing the number of congregations, and more full-time ministry positions reduced to part-time positions. Despite research that indicates some stagnation in enrollment from students in their thirties and forties, an Auburn Seminary study in 2013 indicated that, in addition to increasing enrollment of students over fifty, "enrollments of students in their 20s have increased at a faster rate than most other age cohorts" due perhaps to an increased emphasis on service-learning in their previous education.[25] Schools might do well to consider the unique emotional and psychological landscape of these emerging adults and thereby perhaps increase their competitive edge in recruitment.

Second, emerging adults are undergoing many cognitive changes. Jeffrey Arnett, a developmental psychologist whose research has focused on emerging adulthood, believes that emerging adulthood is not just a failure to grow up but fulfills a purpose as a critical stage for the emergence of the complex forms of thinking required in complex societies.[26] Arnett and others identify significant changes in the emerging adults' sense of self and capacity for self-reflection. The ability of emerging adults for advanced cognitive development is influenced highly by the type of education they received during this period of their lives. At this stage, emerging adults often decide on a particular worldview and are able to recognize that other perspectives exist and are valid as well. This should raise your eyebrows, especially if you teach theology or missiology or pastoral care.

While the emerging adult brain is pruning away unused connections it has made earlier in life and making new connections in a kind of final neural growth spurt, it is also optimizing new learning.[27] There's a reason going back to school is harder the older you get. The adolescent brain is busy pruning or deleting information that it deems irrelevant at the same time that it is solidifying other neurons by wrapping them in myelin, a fatty white tissue that speeds up the ability of the neurons

25. Barbara G. Wheeler, Anthony T. Ruger, and Sharon L. Miller, "Students and Graduates: Theological Student Enrollment," Auburn Seminary, http://www.auburnseminary.org/students-and-graduates?par=838.
26. Jeffrey Jensen Arnett and Jennifer Lynn Tanner, *Emerging Adults in America, Coming of Age in the 21st Century* (Washington, DC: American Psychological Association, 2006).
27. Ferris Jabr, "The Neuroscience of 20-Somethings," *Scientific American* blog, August 29, 2012, http://blogs.scientificamerican.com/brainwaves/2012/08/29/the-neuroscience-of-twenty-somethings/.

to transmit their electrical impulses. This process continues, although much more slowly, into the twenties as the brain develops stronger and stronger bridges that connect the emotional and motor centers with the prefrontal cortex. More than any other characteristic, this increasing interconnectedness describes the emerging adult brain.

If you teach emerging adults in any educational setting, you have a unique opportunity to participate not only in their spiritual and vocation formation, but in their neural formation as well. Emerging adults are seeking connections, building bridges of empathy and compassion that affect decision making, analyzing sensory data and new information, and solidifying their identity and their perspective on the world in relationship to others. Full myelination is probably not reached until around age thirty or maybe even later, according to some neuroscientists,[28] which means that you have an opportunity to help shape what they will remember and, hopefully, what will stick with them as they take their place in the world. But that means you need to understand how memory works.

Make It Stick

What was the most surprising thing you encountered as you read this chapter? What does it make you think of? Did the surprising information connect with anything you already knew or remind you of an educational experience you have had either as a student or an instructor? Reflect on a recent teaching experience. Can you identify something in the planning, curriculum, environment, or assessment you used that reflects how the brain works? Can you identify something that did not effectively reflect how the brain works and what you might do to change that element next time?

---

28. Pat Wolfe, "The Adolescent Brain: A Work in Progress," Mind Matters, Inc., http://patwolfe.com /2011/09/the-adolescent-brain-a-work-in-progress/.

Chapter 4

How Memory Works

Holly J. Inglis

Which came first—the chicken or the egg? The same kind of question could be asked of memory. Which comes first—learning or memory? There are two aspects of memory: *retrieval* and *storage*. A cognitive definition is primarily interested in retrieval, while a biological definition of memory is primarily concerned with how the learned information is stored.

Some educators, as well as cognitive neuroscientists, define memory as learning, using memory as the evidence or assessment of learning and retrieval as the assessment of memory. The purpose of learning is therefore to remember, to retrieve information, and so teaching methods and pedagogy are developed to enhance long-term retention of information. Undoubtedly, we want students to be able to recall information gained in the course of their seminary or religious-studies education, but is that the ultimate goal?

A purely biological definition considers memory to be the pattern of data recorded and stored in the cortex of the brain, which is received as both internal and external sensory stimuli. These stimuli can be conscious or unconscious events, procedures and experiences that excite the neural synapses, causing electrical and chemical responses that have potential to develop various forms of memory.

While the biological definitions are helpful in understanding what is taking place at a specific moment when stimuli is received, memory is no one, single phenomenon, but is instead a variety of different memory systems, interacting with each other and yet independent from one another. Memory, like learning, is not localized, but is distributed widely throughout the brain. From the prefrontal cortex to

---

*QR code URL: http://elearninginfographics.com/how-does-the-brain-retain-information-infographic/.

the cerebellum and in between, your brain is working hard to store data in a variety of ways and places, depending on how it arrives, how you respond, and a host of other factors, some of which become extremely relevant for educators who want the learning experiences to be memorable for their students.

Five Pathways to Memory

The process of developing memory, or identifying and storing the information and experiences that are received by the brain, begins in the memory pathways of the brain. These pathways are like the aisles of your favorite supermarket. Because you shop there frequently, you can generally find the items you want, unless they move the items around or change the layout of the store. Our brain does not change the overall layout of the "store," so these five memory pathways are the consistent aisles our brains use to locate the memories stored throughout our brain. We can access each of these memory pathways intentionally through specific methods or techniques in our teaching, but we can also access them for our own process of remembering and retrieving information.

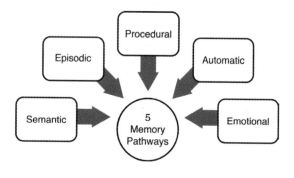

Before we embark on a detailed tour of each memory pathway, stretch out your left hand in front of you with the palm facing up or your right hand with palm facing down, whichever feels most natural. Now take a few minutes to associate each of the memory pathways with your fingers, beginning with your thumb as the semantic memory pathway. Perhaps you prefer to use an acronym to remember the memory pathways: SEPAE. Right now, this information probably does not have much meaning or significance to you, but keep that hand handy and remember which hand you chose as we learn about the five memory pathways.

1. *Semantic memory* holds information learned from words, which can come from lectures, conversations, class discussions, or words on a written page. This pathway is difficult to use for learning because it takes several repetitions of the information to make it stick in the pathway and for long-term storage to take place.

Semantic memory requires repetition in order to stick.

In order for information from words to stick, it must be stimulated by associations, comparisons, and similarities. It could be considered to be one of the least reliable types of memory. It can easily fail us but it does have some good points.

Remember the role of the hippocampus? Like a university library, the hippocampus has access to a wealth of files just waiting to be opened and unlimited capacity to store new factual information, which is primarily word-based information. Making the proper associations can open up any of those files and help retrieve the factual information that you have stored—provided that you have taken steps to associate, compare, and connect new information with previously learned information.

Make It Stick

Stretch out your hand just as you did previously. Wiggle your thumb, which you associated with semantic memory. Now close your eyes and recall the last lecture you attended as a participant. Did you hear anything that was similar to something you have heard before or related to something previously learned (open those hippocampus files)? You are accessing your semantic pathway at the same time you are creating new associations between your finger and the event.

2. *Episodic memory* is much easier to access than the semantic-memory pathway. Episodic memory is contextual memory. It deals with space, locations, or circumstances. You are always located somewhere when you learn something. The route to this pathway is through the hippocampus; location is factual information.

Good educators know that place matters and space teaches. Episodic memory teaches us that the content of the room becomes part of the context of the memory. Beginning as far back as John Dewey, the father of modern education, who noted in 1916 that indirect education occurs through the environment,[1] educational theorists have documented the effect of physical space on academic performance. Educator and consultant Marilee Sprenger refers to physical space as invisible information, an important component of episodic memory that associates place with content.[2] The information the teacher wishes to communicate becomes associated with physical elements of the classroom space, such as the walls, desks, and even the teacher him- or herself. Research has proven that students have more trouble solving math problems when asked to take a math exam in their English classroom than they do when taking the same exam in their math classroom because the walls, desks, whiteboards, and even the teacher are covered with "invisible information." When the student leaves the physical learning space, whether that is a classroom or an online space, the invisible information is no longer present, and the association with the content is weakened. The content of the physical space becomes part of the context of learning and can either contribute to, detract from, or deter the learning. Some educators advocate utilizing the physical learning space as an advance organizer by setting up stimuli that immediately engages the learner's brain in organizing and connecting activity.[3]

---

1. John Dewey, *Democracy and Education* (New York: Macmillan, 1916), 19, quoted in Thomas Groome, *Christian Religious Education* (San Francisco: Jossey-Bass, 1980), 225.
2. Marilee Sprenger, *Learning and Memory: The Brain in Action* (Alexandria, VA: Association for Supervision and Curriculum Development, 1999), 52.
3. Barbara Bruce, *Our Spiritual Brain* (Nashville: Abington, 2002), 94–95.

Make It Stick

Stretch out your hand again, this time wiggling your first finger, which you associated with episodic memory. Where are you located right now? What is the context in which you are reading this section? Slowly look around you. Look for things that might be invisible information, then close your eyes and visualize your context as you wiggle your first finger again. You are accessing and cementing information about episodic memory in your episodic memory pathway.

3. *Procedural memory*, or "muscle memory," as it is often called, stores memories of the processes that the body does routinely, warehousing sequences of muscle movements necessary to replicate an action without receiving new information each time. This is the pathway we use when we are trying to locate an item, like our misplaced keys. We return to where we remember having it last (episodic memory), hoping that our muscle memory will kick in and help us remember what actions we took with the keys. This is how we remember to drive a car, or ride a bicycle, or play a piece on the piano that we have memorized. Our brain stores the information in the cerebellum when the sequence of actions becomes routine.

An interesting fact about procedural memory: if something is learned in a particular position—for example, while sitting at a desk—it is most easily remembered if the individual returns to that position to trigger the memory. These memories involve knowledge that may not be expressed easily in words. When was the last time you explained to someone how to tie shoes? As a matter of fact, if you were tying your shoes and someone asked you, "How do you do that?," it would take a shift away from procedural memory to semantic memory for you to be able to answer their question.

Make It Stick

Stretch out your hand again. This time as you wiggle your second finger, think about something you have learned which is now a habit for you. Close your hand into a fist. Stretch out your hand again and recall something else which is procedural while wiggling the same finger. Repeat this process until you are not able to recall any more things which are part of your procedural memory.

4. *Automatic memory* is considered a "conditioned-response memory." It is called automatic because certain stimuli automatically activate the stored information without having to intentionally do anything to trigger it; think B. F. Skinner and his conditioned response experiments. Like procedural memory, automatic memory is associated with the cerebellum. It may or may not involve muscles, movement, or action, but through repetition and practice these memories, like procedural memories, have become second nature to us. It contains any learning that has become unconscious, such as multiplication skills, the alphabet, or other information that

uses a repetitious learning methodology. If you used flash cards to learn a language, that information is stored in part in your automatic memory.

Automatic memory has the potential to spark other memory lanes to open. For example, if you hear a familiar melody, your automatic memory prompts you to sing along (semantic memory recalls the words), which leads you to remember the last time you sang the song and where you were when you sang it (episodic memory). Perhaps you learned to play this song on an instrument and so your fingers start playing the notes in the air (procedural memory). If you are aware of any feelings associated with any one of these memories, you have opened the door to the last memory pathway.

Make It Stick

By now, you are expecting that I will ask you to stretch out your hand because we have repeated the process three times before. Instead, I want you to start reciting multiplication tables for any number out loud. Begin by multiplying the number by one and continue through ten. Each time you speak, press your third finger, which you associated with automatic memory, firmly onto a nearby surface, such as a table. In a simple way, you are conditioning yourself to remember automatic memory whenever you press your third finger into a surface. When you have completed this exercise, close your fist and open your hand again. See if you can recall the associations you made between each finger and the memory pathways.

5. *Emotional memory* takes precedence over any other kind of memory. The brain gives priority to emotions, in case there is a threat associated with the emotion requiring us to make a fast exit. Sometimes this can result in a form of neuro-hijacking of the brain. When emotions are involved, especially fear, logic may go out the window. As we discussed earlier, emotional memories may cause the release of stress hormones or "feel-good" neurotransmitters, making our behavior strongly connected to the strength of our feelings. The amygdala, you may recall, holds the key to this memory pathway, as the relay station for emotional information. If the emotional stimuli is too strong, the formation of factual memory can actually be blocked by neurochemicals.

Emotional memory trumps all other forms of memory.

Educators, scientists, and theologians agree that the stronger the feeling, the more readily the memory is recalled and the more durable the memory. Jerry Larsen, an ordained United Methodist minister, has written one of the few books connecting religious education and the brain, in which he suggests that when strong emotions are joined with an experience, the combination of information and experience becomes remembered as a word-event[4] and the information and the experience are fused into a single memorable experience. If the experience produces positive, pleasant emotions, research indicates it is likely to be remembered with more detail than experiences that produce negative or unpleasant emotions.

Emotional responses to stimuli are intended to grab our attention. Experts in marketing capitalize on the concept of emotional connection to motivate our consumption. Neuroscientists and educators identify attention-getting and emotional attachment as two crucial ways the brain determines the importance of information and whether or not the information is relevant enough for us to keep. Even John Calvin, the sixteenth-century academic and theologian, recognized the importance of engaging the emotions, the heart, and the soul, along with the mind when he identified the seat of faith in the heart of a believer. In his *Institutes*, Calvin states that, "the word is not received in faith when it merely flutters in the brain, but when it has taken deep root in the heart."[5]

Make It Stick

Time for one last review of the memory device we have created. Take a moment to notice how you are feeling about the information you have read so far. Perhaps something has triggered a memory for you, hopefully associated with a positive emotion. Another option is to recall a recent learning experience that was positively emotionally charged for you. In either case, as you recall the memory, close your eyes and gently massage your pinky finger, which you associated with emotional memory earlier. Just to solidify the memory pathways in your brain, review the association with each finger one more time.

I was involved in parish ministry for over twenty-five years before I discovered what science was revealing about the brain, which led me to surprising new insights about teaching and learning in a congregational setting. The childhood rhyme "Here is the church, here is the steeple" is a good example of how memory applies to the context of parish ministry.

 Scan this QR code for video of this classic rhyme in action.[6]

Make a church with your hands clasped. Recalling the associations you made between each finger and one of the memory pathways, you will notice that your thumbs, or semantic memory, form the door to the church. Word-based memory

4. Jerry Larsen, *Religious Education and the Brain* (Mahwah, NJ: Paulist, 2000), 101.
5. John Calvin, *Institutes of the Christian Religion*, trans. Henry Beveridge (Grand Rapids: Eerdmans, 1994), Bk. 3, ch. 2, sect 36, 501.
6. QR code URL: http://www.youtube.com/watch?v=-H3E33o4URc.

is often the primary memory pathway accessed at church. We are people of the Word, after all. Your first fingers, or episodic memory, form the steeple. Church is always a destination, a location, a place, regardless of whether the space is a camp setting or a storefront or a home or a traditional church building. The other memory pathways—procedural, automatic, and emotional—take place in intentional and unintentional ways as we worship, serve, play, pray, and learn together. Procedural memory includes elements such as kneeling to pray, making the sign of the cross, communion either by intinction or passing trays in the pews, and anything else that involves movement repeated over and over again. Automatic memory includes responses such as "The Lord be with you/And also with you," hearing and seeing the juice or wine poured into the chalice, or other conditioned responses. Emotional memory is powerful in this context and may include such things as feelings about others who worship with you, music, spiritual experiences in that location, being present when a baptism takes place, or sharing stories.[7]

This example raises many questions about what occurs in the context of parish ministry and how it might become stickier for those who worship there. For those in your learning context who intend to move into parish ministry, this is an important conversation. It also elevates the importance of the pedagogy that we use to teach them. Remember: we teach as we are taught! If we want faith formation to be more "sticky" in a church context, then we must teach in ways that use "sticky" pedagogy and encourage students to practice "sticky" teaching, both in the classroom and in their parish as well. Before we move into considering some practical elements of "sticky" teaching and learning, there are a few more features of memory that are essential for us to understand.

Make It Stick

Review the memory pathways in the context of your learning environment by taking a piece of paper and turning it to landscape position. Divide it into five columns and write one of the memory pathways at the top of each column. Reflect on the learning environments you create for your students. How many pathways can you identify? How are the pathways used, either intentionally or unintentionally, to help the information presented stick with your students? Which pathways do you utilize most often? Are there memory pathways that you might consider more in the future, based on what you have read and thought about?

The memory pathways obviously do not work independently of one another, but in concert, to develop multiple ways of remembering and retrieving varieties of information gleaned from a single event. Memory is a stored pattern of connections between neurons in the brain. Every sensation we remember, every thought we think alters the connection in that vast network; our physical substance changes.

---

7. Holly J. Inglis, "Hearers and Doers: Becoming a Whole-Brain Church," D. Ed. Min. thesis, Columbia Theological Seminary, 2012.

The purpose of "sticky" learning is to target the development of memory that sticks with an individual long-term and is able to be retrieved, is meaningful, and becomes transformative as they engage information stored in long-term memory with new information encountered in future contexts.

Why Can't I Remember?

In addition to pathways for the development of memories in the brain, there are different types of memory that behave differently. Memory is composed of three basic types: sensory memory, short-term memory, and long-term memory. Each type of memory varies in what form of information is held, how long the information is held, and the storage capacity.

 For an illustration of the types of memory, go to this link.[8]

1. *Sensory memory* is exactly what you would expect—memory that holds on to information gleaned through the five senses. You walk past a bakery and immediately the smell of delicious baked goods enters through your olfactory nerve, shooting a message to the olfactory cortex, telling you it is the smell of fresh bread. Sensory information can, of course, be good news, like the fresh bread or bad news, like the taste of sour milk on your cereal. But here is the truly bad news about sensory memory: it lasts for less than one second. There is some indication that words and sounds can stick around for a bit longer, perhaps as long as four seconds. As the shortest form of memory, sensory memory can retain the sensory information after the stimuli is gone, but erodes quickly, giving us just enough time to decide if we should pay more attention to the stimuli. And there is no point in trying to work on improving this type of memory. It is just not possible to extend the time that the information is held in the sensory memory. This type of memory is considered by neuroscientists to happen unconsciously and to be beyond our control.

Sensory memory lasts for less than one second.

Try this experiment: choose an object to look at, close your eyes, count to three, then open them, quickly looking at the object, then close them as quickly as you can. What is likely to happen is that after you close your eyes the second time, you will see a shadow image, almost as if it is etched on the inside of your eyelids,

---

8. QR code URL: http://www.human-memory.net/types.html.

but that fades away in a matter of seconds. That is sensory memory. Perhaps this exercise has grabbed your attention, which is the purpose of sensory memory.

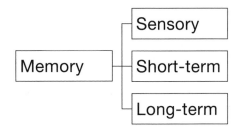

2. *Short-term memory* has slightly better news for us in terms of its stickiness, but don't get too excited yet. Compared to sensory memory, short-term memory sticks much longer: a few seconds up to one minute. Short-term memory is like opening multiple tabs in your Web browser. Right now, I probably have fifteen or more separate tabs open in my browser, but I do not pay attention to any of them for very long and I shift quickly from one to the other. If short-term memory was a video game, you would have one minute to grab the items that fly across the screen in front of you. In the sensory-memory version of the video game, you have less than one second to grab them. Information can move from sensory memory into short-term memory based on our attention. If we are convinced that the information is interesting and deserves our attention, then we filter out other information and ignore other things, placing our attention on that which has captured our interest.

Short-term memory can last up to one minute.

A few years ago, I took a series of exams for ordination after having completed my last seminary class over twenty-five years previously. The first exam consisted of one hundred multiple-choice questions, intended to assess knowledge of stories, themes, and pertinent passages in the Old and New Testaments. To prepare for this examination, I gathered study documents from a variety of sources and reviewed previous exams available online. I attempted to discipline myself to review one exam per day in the weeks preceding the examination, but reality intervened and, as the exam got closer, my strategy shifted. I abandoned studying or reading and focused solely on the online exams, sometimes reviewing five or six exams a day, attempting to memorize the necessary information. I was intentionally cramming, but I knew I had learned the basic material during seminary and I wanted to retrieve information that I knew was in my brain. It did not come easily, but I remembered enough to pass the exam. It was not a very effective learning method because, three years later, I can remember only one piece of information I learned in preparation for the examination, primarily because it seemed relevant.

You can also think of short-term memory as a kind of neuro-sticky note. I would be lost if I didn't keep a notepad by the keyboard in the process of writing this book so that I can write down thoughts that relate to one part of the book as I work on a different part. Sometimes I find it helpful to write my fleeting thoughts on color-coded sticky notes, which I organize on the wall by my desk, based on which part of the book they relate to best. These techniques help me organize and make sense of my thoughts, and later I am able to use them to construct coherent meaning. Without my temporary notes, I would have difficulty remembering my thoughts or processing them and connecting them to my previous knowledge or information.

Short-term memory does have its limits. Most neuroscientists believe there is a seven-item maximum capacity in our short-term memory, although some believe it may be as few as five or six. Not too many years ago, the phone company in my area began to require that we include area codes with phone numbers when dialing. Phone numbers are seven numbers. When you add the area code, there are ten numbers. This is a problem when I try to remember a phone number without writing it down, and even sometimes when I look up a number and turn to write it down. Was the area code 303 or 720? I can't tell you how often I have dialed a number only to get a wrong number because I have the wrong area code. The answer? As many people did, I started shortening the area code to one digit. It is not foolproof, because it still stretches my brain to remember whether it's a 3 or a 7, but my error rate has dramatically decreased.

Short-term memory has a limited capacity and a limited duration. Unless the information is converted into a more robust form of memory, it can vanish, as if it never happened at all. In order to transform a short-term memory into more a permanent form of memory, we must make some assessments about the information. Is this information meaningful to me? Is it relevant? How significant is this information?

Make It Stick

If you just read the words in the preceding paragraph, presumably in silence, go back and read the words out loud to yourself. Why am I suggesting you do this? Because when you read the words out loud, your short-term memory holds on to the words formed by the sounds you make, albeit briefly. If you read the paragraph above out loud several times, you increase the likelihood that it will stick around in your conscious mind. Just like with sensory memory, there's nothing you can do to change the capacity of short-term memory, but there are ways to influence the duration and the stickiness. Rehearsing the information becomes very important in helping to transform short-term memory into long-term memory.

Some neuroscientists equate short-term memory with *working memory*; some suggest working memory is actually a subset of short-term memory, a collection of various temporary memory processes, while others suggest that short-term memory is actually a part of working memory. Most agree on one thing, however: short-term memory temporarily stores information *without* manipulating the information, while working memory combines temporary storage *with* manipulation of the information. Rehearsing the information, as you did by rereading the paragraph above, allows you to manipulate mentally the concepts and ideas, tossing them around unconsciously in your brain in order to determine their relevance, significance, and meaning. Working memory is akin to the desktop of your computer, where you may place a document you are working on rather than embedding it deeply within the file system of your hard drive.

Working memory manipulates information.

Maybe this has happened to you: you are working downstairs and realize that you need something that is located upstairs. In order to remember what you need, you begin repeating it to yourself as you go upstairs. Repetition and rehearsal are important to the function of both short-term and working memory. Short-term memory helps us hold on to something because it is immediately important to us. Working memory helps us hold on to something because we believe it might be important to us in the near future or might be relevant to something we've done before. It is this unique capacity to hold information temporarily that some neuroscientists claim is distinctive to humans.

What happens to the information in our working memory? Again, neuroscientists do not all agree, but most will concur on a few details. First, the prefrontal cortex appears to be involved in both short-term memory and working memory. That may seem odd, based on how the prefrontal cortex functions as the higher, executive-functioning aspect of the brain, but it is precisely that executive role which is involved in the mental juggling of information in working memory and assists in calling up information from other parts of the brain in the assessment process. The prefrontal cortex sorts and sifts the information and, in part, prompts the brain to answer the three questions about meaning, relevance, and significance.

Second, once the information is lost, it is unlikely it will be recovered in either short-term or working memory. There are no memory trails to retrace, like in episodic memory. You didn't "forget" the information, so you cannot recall it. You simply didn't hold on to it. Has this ever happened to you?—You find yourself engaged in a lively discussion with some of your colleagues. One of your colleagues makes a highly debatable point, but before you can respond, another colleague jumps in and begins speaking. Not wanting to appear rude, you wait for your colleague to finish speaking and open your mouth to express your opinion . . . and cannot remember what you were going to say to the first colleague who opened up the debate. You may try reconstructing the argument in your mind, perhaps even pointing to your colleagues as you try to recapture your thoughts, but more often than not, the point you wanted to make is gone.

Third, both short-term memory and working memory have a life-span of a few seconds up to one minute, but the longevity depends on the content, as well as some other factors. It seems that if the pieces of information are even loosely related to one another, rather than disconnected units of information, our brains can hold them easier. Phone numbers are experienced as individual pieces of information. Six or seven words that relate to one another, however, are not perceived as individual units, but more as a unified whole.

Make It Stick

Take a moment to look at the list of numbers below, then cover them up with your hand and see if you can correctly recall them.
63-14-2-31-47-9-50
Now take a moment to look at the series of words below, then cover them up and see if you can correctly recall them.
Pentecost-Advent-Easter-Epiphany-Lent-Christmas-Ordinary
If I am correct, the second list was easier for you to recall than the first list, even if you were unable to get the second list completely correct.

When your brain encounters information like these lists, the first thing it does is to begin to look for patterns and for familiar information. If it detects something recognizable, your brain can start to get excited and neurons start to fire. However, there are a couple of other factors that can derail this process. Working memory is very fragile, so any slight distraction can jar the information from your working memory. Activities that require switching attention from one thing to another will accelerate the loss of information as well. Once again, repetition and rehearsal increase the possibility of holding the information.

3. Both sensory memory and short-term (working) memory are in the realm of *temporary memory*, or memory that has not yet become *permanent memory*. *Long-term memory* has far greater storage capacity, is more durable, and robust. Long-term memory is considered to be permanent, to last for a lifetime. Neurologic pruning will remove some connections over time if they are unused, but, for the most part, when we talk about sticky learning, we are talking about learning that can last a lifetime.

Long-term memory lasts a lifetime and can hold facts, events, experiences, concepts, skills, and tasks.

The hippocampus is the catalyst for long-term memory, but the actual memory is distributed throughout the brain; the location depends on the type of information involved in the memory. Long-term memory has both *declarative memory* (facts, events, experiences, concepts) and *procedural memory* (skills, tasks) and each get created slightly differently. Since most of what we do in traditional education is declarative and deals with events, experiences, facts, and concepts, here is an overly simplified explanation of how long-term declarative memory is formed.

Information about events, experiences, facts, and concepts is received by different parts of the brain. These bits of information, decoded by the various sensory areas of the cortex, get routed through the hippocampus, the reference librarian, which triggers the search for prior matching information. The hippocampus knows where the previously stored information is located, retrieves it, and shuttles it, along with the new information, back into temporary storage areas in each lobe to be examined. If the prior information connects to the new information, it is sent to the working memory in the prefrontal cortex. Unless it gets distracted, working memory will continue to sort and sift the old and new material, provided the prefrontal cortex judges it to be relevant, interesting, significant, and worth our attention. Because of our prior knowledge, our attention, or interest, the new information may be added to the old and form a stronger memory. Every time this process is repeated, the hippocampus strengthens the associations. With enough repetitions, it no longer has to work as hard to solidify the connection, because the synaptic connections have been reinforced. The cortex, where the hippocampus sends the strengthened information, has "learned" to make its own associations. This process may have to be repeated several times before long-term memory is actually formed. If emotion or feelings are associated with the sensory input, then the amygdala declares that the information will *definitely* be remembered and trumps all other forms of memory. Just remember, if something distracts you in the midst of this process or you lose interest or are doing too many things at one time, the information can disappear from working memory, and you will need to start all over again. It's a wonder we ever remember anything at all!

If you are not able to remember all the steps in this process, perhaps it will be easier for you to remember this six-word descriptive phrase: *Cells that fire together, wire together!* Long-term potentiation theory (LTP) suggests that every time a neuron fires information across a synapse, the memory of that information is encoded exponentially; the information is learned multiple times each time it is practiced. The signal changes the potentiality of the receiving neuron. Because the neuron has been excited or stimulated by the information once, it now has the potential to receive that information faster. If the receiving neuron does not get the same information within about ninety minutes, it will reset itself to zero and act as if nothing happened.[9] Long-term potentiation is an example of synaptic plasticity, or the brain's ability to change and grow. Once thought not to be true, indeed, it appears that you actually can "change your mind."

There is one more, somewhat disturbing fact about memory that you need to know before we begin considering what all this means for our classrooms and other learning experiences. According to studies conducted by Northwestern University, your memories are changed each and every time you recall them.[10] When you recall something, you are not actually recalling the memory. Instead, you are recalling your memory of the memory, or a reconstruction of the memory. Every time

9. John Medina, *Brain Rules* (Seattle: Pear Press, 2008), 135.
10. Marla Paul, "Your Memory Is Like the Telephone Game," Northwestern University, http://www
.northwestern.edu/newscenter/stories/2012/09/your-memory-is-like-the-telephone-game.html.

you assemble the pieces of a memory from the various parts of your brain, you are recalling the memory from the last time you stored it, and every time you retrieve the memory, the accuracy degrades just a little bit. Donna Bridge, a postdoctoral fellow at Northwestern and lead author on an article in the *Journal of Neuroscience*, goes so far as to say that it is possible that your memory can grow less and less precise over time to the point of being completely inaccurate. Furthermore, when your memory of an event begins to develop holes or gaps in the information, your creative brain will work its hardest to fill in the gaps. Because the brain is always seeking to make meaning and sense of the world, we use the frameworks and knowledge already embedded in our brains to fill in the gaps and conjecture what might have happened. This predictive schema steps in to fill in the gaps in a reconstructed memory, more often times than not with inaccurate information that it believes fits with the memory.

The implications for legal proceedings are obvious. Eyewitness accounts of crimes have been used countless times to send accused perpetrators to jail, only to discover later that the eyewitness was inaccurate or sometimes blatantly wrong. These individuals weren't lying. They were simply demonstrating the "you-can't-step-into-the-same-river-twice" principle of memory. Every time these witnesses were asked by detectives, lawyers, or anyone else to recall what happened, they were reshaping the memory, more details were falling away, and the reconstructed memory was re-encoded in the brain. But what are some implications of this aspect of memory for theological and religious-studies education?

Disrupt Pathways to Enhance Learning

One of the first things students learn in biblical interpretation is that the canon was not written down as it was occurring. They learn how oral tradition dominated ancient Near Eastern cultures and that people lived for stories, especially stories that established meaning and order to their world. We explain the concept of textual variants and the possibility that scribes made slight alterations either intentionally or unintentionally as they copied the sacred texts, but we do not usually talk about how the people would have remembered the stories and how the process of retelling produces slight alternations in the story. The Gospels provide a good example of this process of reconstructive memory. Biblical scholars are not in general agreement about whether the Gospels were written by direct witnesses or those who knew the witnesses or those who were friends of those who knew the witnesses. While not negating the authority or truth of Scripture in any sense, we understand that the Gospel writers were not primarily concerned with the precise accuracy of the eyewitnesses. They were, for the most part, relying on the reconstructive memory of their sources. Their purpose was not to create a documentary about Jesus' life and ministry but, rather, to paint a portrait that led people to understand who Jesus was and to accept him as the Son of God, hence the distinctions between the Gospels, the inclusion of different stories about Jesus, and differences between writers who include the same stories. No judge in a court of law would likely accept accounts of events that happened thirty to sixty years ago, yet this is precisely what the Gospels contain.

Sharing this information with your students may elicit some strong responses. For some students, who may approach Scripture as a unilateral eyewitness account of God's activity throughout history, you are creating some cognitive dissonance, which can be unsettling. You may hear responses such as, "But in my undergraduate religion class I learned . . . ," or "My Sunday school teacher taught me . . . ," or even "My pastor told me . . ." If you encounter resistance or even anger when presenting concepts such as these, know that you are asking your students to reorganize their thinking and quite possibly disrupting a memory that may be deeply embedded, but as we will encounter in the next section, disturbing memory patterns with new information is key to memorable learning. When our minds are "changed" by repeated experiences that disturb or shake up our previously held patterns of thought, we have the possibility of not just transforming our brains, but our actions and behavior as well.

Part Three

The Courage to Change the Things You Can

Read what my medal says: "Courage."
Ain't it the truth? Ain't it the truth?
—The Cowardly Lion, *The Wizard of Oz*

Chapter 5

Tips for Sticky Learning

Holly J. Inglis

I n the 1939 film *The Wizard of Oz*, the tornado deposits Dorothy's house at the beginning of the Yellow Brick Road, which eventually leads her and her companions to the Emerald City in the Land of Oz. You may not have noticed this, particularly if you have viewed the film in black and white, but there is another road, a red brick road, that can be spotted starting at the same point as the Yellow Brick Road but going in a different direction. You may also recall that after Dorothy meets the Scarecrow, there is a three-way fork in the road and together they decide which road to take. As we head off on our journey into the Land of Sticky Learning, know that there will be choices along the way. Given what you have read so far, you may have already decided that this journey is not for you. If you are intrigued and interested in following this path, you will have opportunities to choose what may or may not fit for you or what you are willing and not willing to try.

Sticky learning depends on many things. Content delivery is one of the most important aspects of sticky learning. The way in which information is delivered, who delivers it, and what form the information takes are all important considerations if we want to encourage our students to remember what they learn. We want our students to be excited about learning in part because when they are excited then we are excited. We know that, in reality, sometimes neither one of us is very excited about what is happening in the learning context. I have distilled some of the most well-respected brain-based teaching and learning information into five factors that seem most relevant to religious education and which, I believe, are

---

*QR code URL: https://www.youtube.com/watch?v=6LIhIJMkqnE. This QR code points to an overview of sticky learning via an original song written by Chris Peters, M.Div., for an "Introduction to Christian Education class at Columbia Theological Seminary," October 2013.

worthy of discussion with your colleagues and across disciplines. I believe they have the potential to excite your students about learning as well as excite you about teaching. We will examine each of these factors and then pause to allow you time to process and apply the information to your particular situation. The five tips for sticky learning are intended to spark your imagination about what you teach, how you teach, and even who is doing the teaching.

While content and information is certainly a key element of formal learning that takes place in traditional educational settings with overt curriculum, we should not negate the variety of informal settings in which learning also takes place. The coffee shop, living room, carpool, gym, any of the places where your students interact are equally capable of sticky learning. To affect learning in the informal setting, you need to make the formal setting sticky. Sticky learning also has broader applications than a formal classroom setting. The concepts can infuse the hidden curriculum (the organizational design, room arrangement, grading structure) and the concomitant curriculum (that which is taught or emphasized at home, at church, or in social experiences). Paying more attention to all the ways and places in which we learn and how our brains create memories increases the potential that all of us, teachers as well as students, will develop rich, robust understandings that can transform our actions. Transformative learning is our Oz, the land we seek. So off we go!

Five Tips for Sticky Learning/Sticky Teaching

1. Stimulate more senses; vision trumps all senses

The senses are the loading docks of the brain, delivering loads of information to our brain. But not all of our senses are treated equally. The brain devotes more neurons and more of the cortex area to receiving and processing visual information than any other sense.[1] If you took a poll of your students, it is likely that more than 75 percent of them would declare that they are visual learners. In fact, approximately 25 percent of brain activity is devoted to visual perception, followed by auditory perception at a distant second. If vision trumps all the other senses, why bother to stimulate more senses? The more of our senses we engage, the greater the likelihood that the information will be more elaborately encoded. The more senses that are involved, the deeper the memory path is embedded.[2] Our senses were designed to work in concert with one another, so that in the caves or savannahs of the ancient world, we could create an instantaneous picture of the world around us in order to assess our surroundings and situation. Our senses were intended to work together for our survival. In the same way, a multisensory learning experience grabs the attention of your learners and may possibly spark the attention of more of your students than simply using one sense, such as sound. Remember the image of aisles in a grocery store that we used when we introduced the concept of the five memory pathways? Stimulating more of the senses in your classroom is like shopping on multiple aisles at once. As the pathways interconnect, the stimulation

---

1. Jerry Larsen, *Religious Education and the Brain* (Mahwah, NJ: Paulist, 2000), 59.
2. Peter Atkins, *Memory and Liturgy* (Brookfield, VT: Ashgate, 2004), 17.

of one area stimulates related areas and increases the patterning and encoding of the information.

We receive most of our sensory data through what we see and hear, and this is especially true in most educational settings. The power of visuals is undeniable. If you think we see with our eyes, you would be technically incorrect. It is our brains that actually "see" the visual images which our eyes receive through the retina and then send on to our occipital lobes at the back of our brain and other areas of the brain for processing, recognition, and interpretation. Our brain processes visuals sixty thousand times faster than we process text because data from text is received sequentially, like you are reading from left to right across this page.[3] Reading is one of the slowest ways to get data into the brain, while data from visuals is processed instantaneously. We see an image and then we think about the image. Researchers at MIT describe this idea as vision-finding concepts.[4] Hearing verbal information leads our brain to produce its own images of what is being described, but seeing images intentionally chosen to communicate information speaks far louder than words and allows our brain to focus its energy on processing the image rather than having to create its own or search for something similar stored in long-term memory. In October of 2011, I led a small group of adults on a worktrip to Joplin, Missouri, only five months after a devastating tornado ripped through the town. I read magazine articles and news reports to get prepared to lead this trip, but no words could communicate like the visual images we saw. Some of the trip participants remarked, "I didn't think it was this bad" and "Having seen it first-hand, I understand better." Seeing *is* believing, or at least it is a powerful tool for learning and memory.

Chip Heath, a professor of organizational behavior, and his brother, Dan Heath, a business consultant, say that naturally sticky ideas are full of concrete images. John Medina echoes the Heaths' idea and offers specific suggestions for multimedia presentations, based on the work of cognitive psychologist Richard Mayer.[5] Mayer's research on multimedia and learning is clear. People who receive information through a multisensory approach always have better and more precise recall than those who receive the same information through a unisensory approach. Not only that, but the recall persists for several years. Creativity and the ability to problem-solve also improves in a multisensory learning environment, according to Mayer. Is your classroom unisensory or multisensory? As a way to assess your environment, imagine being a student in your class without each one of the senses. Which senses are most necessary for participation in your learning environment? What would you learn and how would you learn it?

Simply using more visual images is not enough to make information stick with your students. More is not better! If you use multimedia or presentation software

3. Rick Blackwood, *The Power of Multi-sensory Preaching and Teaching* (Grand Rapids: Zondervan, 2008), 15.

4. Sarah Griffiths, "Your Brain Really IS Faster Than You Think," *Mail Online*, http://www.dailymail.co.uk/sciencetech/article-2542583/Scientists-record-fastest-time-human-image-takes-just-13-milliseconds.html.

5. John Medina, *Brain Rules* (Seattle: Pear Press, 2008), 208–210.

in your classroom, here are some suggestions that keep in mind our first tip for sticky learning.

- Reduce the number of words on a slide to no more than thirty. Eliminate extraneous material so that brains won't have to work so hard to take in the visual, word-based information. Work at reducing or eliminating multimedia presentations that are exclusively word based. Medina calls a class that uses exclusively heavily loaded, word-based slide presentations "death by PowerPoint."

- Consider using nonlinear presentation software, such as Prezi, which provides a storyboard approach, rather than traditional PowerPoint, which is text based. Both tools allow for integration of images, videos, animations, and sounds, so you have no excuse for only using words in either case.

- If you use visual images, make sure they clearly connect to your intended point and do not detract from your point. If the images are poorly done or do not connect clearly to your point, learner's brains will be more focused on trying to make sense of the image and trying to determine meaning than on the point you are trying to make in your verbal presentation.

- Keep your visual images to a minimum. Remember how short our short-term memory is? Visual short-term memory is just as short *and* has a limit of about four items. Some researchers say this limit is even decreasing. The more complex the image, the fewer images can be held in short-term memory and working memory. Find one or two relevant, moderately complex images and you will do more to help your students learn than with six or eight images. Once again, more is not necessarily better.

- Combine corresponding words and pictures concurrently rather than consecutively. If you use images and words on the same slide, place them close together so the connection is clear. Better yet, unless it is clearly evident, label the images so the students do not have to waste time and focus trying to figure it out.

- If you use animated multimedia, such as YouTube videos, let the animation speak for itself. Allow time to watch the animation, then follow it up with your own narration. This has proven to be more effective and engaging than on-screen text following an animated presentation.

During a visit to an introductory Old Testament seminary classroom, this is what I observed. The professor began by instructing the students to pull up the class notes on their computers from the learning-management system (LMS) course site. As he began to lecture on the book of Job, the students seemed focused on the prewritten, outlined notes. Some added their own notes. Since much of the book of Job circulates around a terrible locust plague, the professor referenced a handout from the previous week and began to read that same handout out loud to the students. Several of the students were busy thumbing through their handouts from the class trying to locate the correct one, while he was busy reading aloud. Finally, after a so-far highly auditory class, the professor told the class that he had placed a link to a YouTube video of a locust plague in Africa on the LMS. He did not show the video in class but invited them to view it later. You can imagine what most of the students did at that point. Several students within my eyeshot immediately connected to the online link and began viewing the video while the professor continued to lecture. Others used a search engine to view images of locusts. Maybe this sounds like a classroom you know. This method of teaching is replicated over and over every day in classrooms across the country. Simple changes in the use of visual stimulation in balance with auditory presentations could improve the stickiness of this Old Testament class.

Make It Stick

Here is your opportunity to practice stimulating more of the senses in your classroom. Take the suggestions for multimedia presentations and imagine how you might present these concepts to your students that is not primarily word based and that follow the suggestions for use of visual images. Remember to begin by looking for natural connections to the five senses.

Of course, all these suggestions are still utilizing only vision and hearing. What if you added an olfactory sense to your educational experience? The sacraments are a great illustration of how a multisensory experience can create memory. While the words and the gestures of the liturgist convey meaning and tell us something important is occurring, it is our physical senses of taste, touch, and smell that create the long-lasting recall of the experience. The last sensory connection to memories to fade is sight and smell,[6] both of which are employed in the celebration of the sacraments. Smells trigger the amygdala. That's why neuroscientists know that smells connect best with emotional memory and autobiographical memory, a combination of personal experiences, people, and events experienced in a particular location. It is undoubtedly a bit trickier to incorporate appropriate smells into a classroom, but are there times where you might trigger some amygdalae or encourage your students to trigger the amygdalae of their peers during class presentations?

Effective use of sensory stimulation begins with your imagination; as you prepare your next lecture or presentation look for points of sensory connection. Enter the material using all your own senses. What sounds, sights, smells, tastes, and elements of touch do you sense? For many disciplines, the sensory element may be difficult, if not impossible to ascertain. Professors who teach courses that use sacred texts can encourage students to look for multisensory gateways as they read the text. In that case, look to your students themselves to provide the multisensory elements, and, in particular, the visual element. Barbara Bruce advises teachers to

6. Larsen, *Religious Education*, 107.

encourage students to doodle or draw images that increase their understanding and make connections. Other possibilities include the use of Venn diagrams or mind maps or other graphic organizers to rehearse auditory information from a lecture. Above all, you do not want the sensory aspects of your learning environment to consume the focus of your students' attention so that they are even less engaged. Make sure your room is sensorial-y satisfactory before class begins. Check the temperature, the seating arrangement and spacing if movable, sunlight or any other sensory elements that might become distractions. Consider also the value of education that happens outside the classroom. Do you recall my experience of the cafeteria discussions during seminary? Perhaps meeting with small groups of students for a follow-up discussion to class in a sensory-loaded setting such as a coffee shop or bakery may enhance their learning and memory and provide an emotional connection to you as well.

2. Connect to prior knowledge

We know our students do not come to our institutions as blank slates. They come with a lifetime (whether that is twenty-two years or fifty-five years) of knowledge and experiences. Prior knowledge is anything your students already know from previous educational experiences, independent learning, or life experiences. Prior knowledge is a sticky hook for new information *if* either you or your students make the connection. This concept is pretty simple, at least in theory, but a bit more complicated to achieve. The research is clear, however; in order for new information to be more easily processed, it needs to be associated with information already present in the learner's brain.[7] Remember, the brain is always searching for meaning and patterns. When new information is presented, the brain begins its task of seeking patterns within previously encoded information or experiences. In fact, it seems that our brains prefer to use patterns already established rather than to build new patterns. To maximize current learning in hopes of turning it into long-term memory, professors need to hook into the information already stored in the long-term memory of students. This process begins by assessing students' prior knowledge in order to intentionally build a bridge between new and existing information. But how does this work?

Use the "Muddy Waters" exercise as an assessment tool. Ask students to write down the muddiest point in today's lecture or reading. Collect the responses then use them to inform the next class.

Educational consultant Willy Wood says that the first step is to find out what your students know and already have in their long-term memory. Short of giving

---

7. Medina, *Brain Rules*, 115; Atkins, *Memory and Liturgy*, 15.

an entrance examination to your class, what options are there for assessing prior long-term memory? Dr. Michelle Jackson at the University of Texas begins each class by asking students to write a one-page response to the question, "What do you know about_____?"[8] Near the end of the semester, she returns the papers and has them respond to their previous writing. She finds students are generally surprised by what they thought they knew and by what they have learned throughout the course. This is only one form of Classroom Assessment Techniques (CATs) that require student participation but are led by the instructor, provide both students and teacher ungraded feedback, and allow the instructor to adjust and shape the content based on the results. Assessing prior knowledge can also highlight misinformation that has become long-term memory. It may be particularly important for those who teach in biblical studies to uncover interpretations that have stuck from earlier learning experiences in church, Sunday school, or parochial school. Knowing your students may be encountering new information allows you to assess the amount of instruction necessary and direct your instruction toward correcting any misinformation. If the new information presented in your class conflicts too greatly with the preexisting misinformation, it can impede the learning and short-circuit any development of memory if the brain determines the information is not relevant.

More examples of CATs.[9]

What if your course assumes no prior knowledge? Just because your course description states that prior knowledge of the subject is not necessary for the class does not mean that your students do not come with some prior knowledge. It may help the learning stick better if you can guide your students to find things in their own experience that connect with concepts you will teach. For example, in a theology course, when considering doctrines of the faith such as grace, begin by asking students if they know anything about grace. When have they ever extended grace to someone or experienced grace from someone? Ask them to describe what happened and to identify characteristics of their experience or characteristics of grace. There are examples throughout church history of theologians, like Augustine, who began their work out of their own spiritual experiences. Whenever possible, highlight the life experiences of theologians that informed their thinking and their work. Allowing students to share their connecting experiences in class can also benefit the emotional memory and perhaps might spark some additional memories.

---

8. Michelle Jackson, "Prior Knowledge Check," BYU Center for Teaching and Learning, http://ctl.byu.edu/teaching-tips/prior-knowledge-check.
9. QR code URL: http://teachingcommons.depaul.edu/Classroom_Activities/classroom_assessment_techniques.html.

Advance organizers (AOs) are yet another way to engage prior knowledge. An AO is information presented prior to formal learning that can be used to help learners organize and process new upcoming information. They function like an appetizer before dinner. David Ausubel is one of the foremost authorities on the use of advance organizers and suggests there are two primary kinds of AOs: *comparative* organizers and *expository* organizers.[10] Comparative organizers are taps on the shoulder to stored information in the working and long-term memory and allow learners to relate what is already known with the new information. To capture students' attention for a new topic, begin by highlighting things they may already know that connect to the new information. If there is no previous knowledge of a subject or topic, expository organizers give information, vocabulary, and structure that will be needed to understand the upcoming new information. Your classroom space can become an advance organizer if you set up pictures, props, or even music that connects with the new topic. By setting up stimuli that immediately engage the learner's brain you are inviting your students to begin organizing and connecting activity as they enter the learning space. Short video clips are another effective expository organizer, such as the one highlighted at the beginning of the section on the brain. By the way, telling your students why you are helping them connect to prior knowledge is a good idea as well and may help them understand the value of the concept to their future vocational settings.

Just as providing an appropriate image allows our brain to focus its energy on processing the image rather than having to create its own, connecting to prior knowledge allows the brain to use its energy on strengthening the linkages between the information, rather than having to forge new neural connections from scratch. Without help to connect new information to prior knowledge, the learner has to work much harder to process the new stimuli/information. Learners may simply tune out because of the heavy demand placed on the short-term capacity to hold the new information if it does not perceive it has any connections. Remember from our earlier discussion that short-term memory is believed to be able to hold a limited amount of information: only seven items simultaneously. By making connections to what the student already knows, you also ease the demand on the student's brain to establish meaning. The more frequently a neural network is accessed, the stronger it becomes. It is similar to lifting weights. It is much easier to lift a weight when the muscles have been built up. Connecting to prior information is using the connections that have already been built up in the brain.

Once you have a sense of what your students may or may not know about the new subject, you will need to create a bridge from the current knowledge to the new information. Wood calls this approach to education "Theirs to Ours, Ours to Theirs."[11] It looks like this: teachers enter their students' world through the portal of the students' previous knowledge and interest and then guide students to make

10. Jeanine M. Dell'Olio and Tony Donk, *Models of Teaching: Connecting Student Learning with Standards* (Thousand Oaks, CA: Sage, 2007), 393–94.

11. Willy Wood, "Seven Steps to Magical Memory," "Learning and the Brain" conference proceedings, Boston, MA, November 22, 2009, 348.

the connections between the prior knowledge (their world) and the new information (our world). Now we need to guide students to apply their new understanding to new situations that are relevant to their life and/or ministry contexts (their world again).

Learning becomes sticky when new information snags knowledge stored in long-term memory. The key is that it doesn't always happen naturally. I love fishing. The image of snagging information connects to my efforts at fishing. Believe me, the fish won't just jump on the hook by themselves. It takes work, having the appropriate bait, and some intelligence about what you are fishing for and what the obstacles might be. There is a wide variety of bait available for you to use in this fishing expedition for prior knowledge: words written or spoken, experiences, relationships, art and visual images, aroma, taste, sounds and music, problems encountered, stories, celebrations, skills gained, concrete objects, and don't forget physical space. When we do theological and religious education, we need to cast knowledge out to our students with as many hooks as possible. What kind of bait is in your tackle box?

Make It Stick

Identify a subject or new information presented in your class. What kind of prior knowledge, if any, might your students have about the subject? Where might they have obtained their prior knowledge? Have there been any occasions when your students may have encountered similar or related information in your class? How might the new information connect with information they have encountered in other classes? Is there something in their life experience you could draw on that might connect? Be careful. If you try to make a connection to their life experience be sure you make it relevant. In the Old Testament class I observed, the professor was trying to make a connection between Job and the life experience of the students by asking how many of them grew up on a farm. Only one or two students raised their hands. His effort to connect Job-locust-farms did not connect with either the experience or the prior knowledge of the majority of his students.

3. Emotional memory trumps all other forms of memory

If vision is the king of the senses, then emotional memory is the queen of all types of memory. Our brains retain items of information that significantly engage one or more of our senses *and* evoke strong feelings. Emotions are like spices: sadness, love, joy, surprise, and anger get stirred into experiences, creating a unique flavor and providing meaning. It seems we are created to feel as well as think, not only for our survival, but so that we may learn about our environment.

Emotional connections answer the "Why is this important?" question. Far from being manipulative or coercive, tapping into emotional memory is a powerful hook for new information. Emotional connection is a form of affective elaboration and helps to establish relevance. Educators, scientists, and theologians all agree that the stronger the feeling, the more easily the memory is recalled and the more durable the memory. Emotion inspires caring and empathetic understanding, which in turn can motivate action. Helping students in a homiletics, preaching, or worship class to understand the appropriate role of emotion in memory can greatly enhance the experience for those whom they will lead.

Our ability to view the world through the eyes of others is rooted not only in the emotional structures of the brain, but also in a vast array of other areas of the brain, including something called mirror neurons that help us tune into each other's emotions. Actors that are really good at their craft can elicit our emotions by putting feeling and drama into their faces and bodies, using their movements to inspire feeling and emotional connection. Experts in marketing also understand how to capitalize on the concept of emotional connection to motivate consumption, but emotion can also motivate expressions of generosity, compassion, and concern, which we would all like to see in those around us, especially among those in our congregations.

 This PBS *Nova* site can help you learn more about mirror neurons.[12]

Because the emotion centers of our brain receive information slightly before the thinking centers, an emotional connection is an attention-grabbing device if applied effectively. Recall in our earlier discussion of emotional memory that once emotional strategies capture our attention, other memory-storage areas are activated, thereby improving the possibility that the new experience will "stick." James McGaugh at the Center for the Neurobiology of Learning and Memory at the University of California, Irvine, suggests that emotional-arousal events are best remembered the next day.[13] McGaugh's study demonstrates the positive effect that showing either positively or negatively emotionally laden pictures before a particularly boring speech or lecture can have on memory. Some neuro-savvy educators go so far as to suggest that without active emotional engagement, although learning can still occur, it may occur more slowly and will require increased stimulation of other memory pathways. Remember, too, that learners do not enter your classroom as emotional blank slates; their learning may be hindered because we do not first address the emotions and emotional memory they bring with them before attempting to engage the learners with new emotionally connecting experiences or information.

While emotional memory is one of the easiest to trigger and will trump all other forms of memory, it is also somewhat of an art form to create an appropriate emotional trigger or learning experience without becoming emotionally

---

12. QR code URL: http://www.pbs.org/wgbh/nova/body/mirror-neurons.html.
13. James L. McGaugh, "Memory Consolidation and the Amygdala," lecture, "Learning and the Brain" conference, Boston, MA, November 22, 2009.

manipulative. We must be cautious that we do not elicit emotion for emotion's sake. Because emotional memory is so strong, if the trigger is too strong and elicits a fear response, it can actually block formation of factual memory. The emotion must always serve the message.

In a polity, theology, or worship course, invite students to recall personal experiences that connect to doctrines or concepts. For example, you might invite your students to recall a significant baptism in their own lives as you begin a study of baptism. Baptisms are an emotionally laden corporate event, and recalling a personal experience of baptism will create an emotional connection to the information. In the same way, inviting congregants to recall a significant baptism in their own lives or in the life of their family before beginning an infant baptism may create a more emotional connection to the individual being baptized, resulting in a stronger connection between the individual and the church and greater investment of the members in the spiritual nurture of the individual. It is the emotions that are awakened that make this type of event easier to remember more than even its personal significance.

Encountering emotion in most pastoral-care situations is expected, but often focuses on fears. To understand more about emotion, fear, and anxiety, see *Redeeming Fear: A Constructive Theology for Living into Hope* by Jason C. Whitehead.[14]

Remember, too, that emotion can be triggered simply by how learners feel about their peers, how they interpret the class experience, how confident they feel about their own knowledge and competency, or how safe the environment feels. If we do not recognize the role feelings and emotional responses play in the classroom, we are short-circuiting the learning process and the potential for sticky learning. Theological education and religious studies, by their very nature, are not merely an exercise of the head, but of the heart and the passion as well. By recognizing how emotions can positively charge learning, we can avoid sterilizing our educational systems of the ardor and zeal we desire for our students to possess and to pass on to others in their ministry.

Story is also an excellent way of creating emotional connection, either through individual stories or a collective story that is part of the shared history of a group. When we hear a story, our brain creates images to accompany the story, sometimes even if the story contains its own pictures. When we tell our own stories, there are episodic and emotion-laden images associated with that story as well. The human brain is wired to organize experiences, including memory of events and the emotional states that connect them, into stories. Why not maximize our

---

14. Jason C. Whitehead, *Redeeming Fear: A Constructive Theology for Living into Hope*, Prisms (Minneapolis: Fortress Press, 2013).

capacity for visual memory and emotional connection through the use of story? Music is another powerful tool for emotional memory. Richard Tietze at Marymount Manhattan College, along with other colleagues, proposes some interesting uses of music in an adult-education context. Since music is such a natural part of our faith, our worship, and plays an important role throughout Scripture, it may be easier to find ways to incorporate appropriate music as an emotional connection in your discipline. Tieze suggests some practical ways music can enhance adult learning. Music can be used to reenergize a classroom or provide a novel way to begin a class, marking a transition from a more passive mode of learning to a more active or interactive mode. Music can encourage playfulness, creativity, and reduce stress. Music can tell a personal story of identity or a story outside the individual.

 Music as a Resource for the Adult Education Experience.[15]

While a single emotional event or response can certainly become etched in our memory, the most robust emotional memories are those that demonstrate affective elaboration. Elaboration, or the extent to which a memory is dispersed throughout the brain, depends on the strength of the feeling attached to the experience and if the emotional experience is rehearsed. Remember that the amygdala is a key player in this game of emotional memory, and dopamine, released by the amygdala at the first hint of emotions, functions like a neuro-sticky note on the piece of information associated with the emotion. Perhaps this explains why emotionally charged events are generally recalled with slightly more accuracy than those where emotion was not highly active. Retelling, recalling, and reenacting the experience along with the information associated with the experience aids the transition from working memory to long-term memory. With the passage of time, however, the details are reduced to more of the gist of the emotional experience.

Emotionally charged events do not always need to take place in the classroom to affect the memory of a classroom experience. Sometimes, it may be advantageous to have students call to mind a common, universal experience that occurred in the recent or not-so-recent past. You must be confident, however, that all the students will be able to relate to the experience, so choose an experience which has broad appeal across generations, genders, and ethnicities. Examples might include natural disasters or tragedies such as the 9/11 attacks as a way of engaging students in a theological examination of evil or violence or, conversely, using celebrations such as the Olympics to begin a discussion on human versus divine judgment.

---

15. QR code URL: http://www.nyu.edu/frn/publications/new.faces.new.expectations/Tietze.html.

Make It Stick

Without becoming manipulative, or sacrificing the integrity of your course content, how can you enhance the emotional environment of your class? Here are a few ideas:

- *Old Testament*: Divide the class into twelve groups for the twelve tribes. As you progress through the course, create emotional tension between the tribes as indicated in Scripture and other source material. Divide the tribes according to the two kingdoms. Seek to help them understand the role each tribe played in the story of Israel through emotional affiliation and connection. Another option is to create groups within the class that reflect the various cultures the Hebrew people encountered in their journey to the promised land and invite them to try and understand the emotions each might have felt as they confronted this monotheistic band of people.

- *Church History and Theology*: Whenever you teach about a conflict or controversy, divide the class into the opposing sides or parties and ask them to argue their perspective on the issue. As a group, invite them to find or create a theme song that illustrates the primary argument or cause for which they fought.

- *New Testament*: Ask students to identify emotional encounters in the texts and to be aware of their own emotional responses as they read. This is good practice for preparing to preach in a way that engages the hearers' emotions as well as their intellect and their spirit.

- *Pastoral Care*: Story is an effective tool for creating emotional memory in pastoral care. Personal narratives from your students can help emphasize a point and illustrate how we make meaning from the stories of our lives. Case studies, movies, novels, and other media can provide narrative content and connections to our emotional life. Role playing provides the chance for students to develop their empathetic skills by engaging in a process that accesses personal memories from an impersonal perspective. Teach your students about the role emotional memory plays in spiritual healing and assisting us as we define ourselves and discover who we are. Because pastoral care often deals with personal stories that have emotional impact, teachers should monitor how students are responding emotionally to particular teaching moments and help them find resources outside of class for monitoring the emotional impact of specific lectures, case studies, and so forth.

- *Worship*: David Hogue, professor of pastoral counseling and theology at Garrett-Evangelical Seminary, writes that both worship and pastoral care are built on a foundation of memory, and emotional memory in particular.[16] Imagination, memory, and story are woven together in the ritual and practice of worship, which Hogue calls an intentional act of remembering. Teaching students about worship and liturgy in memorable ways and teaching students ways to create worship experiences that evoke memories has great potential to be transformative for the students as well as for those to whom they may minister.

- *Homiletics and Preaching*: Instruct students on the neuroscience of emotional memory and encourage them to incorporate the information as your students take turns preaching. The proclamation element of worship is a primary place where emotional memory can be tapped as well as created if done effectively. Encourage students to identify any emotions present in the selected text and then to consider appropriate ways to communicate the emotion.

- *Small Groups*: The use of intentional, structured small groups in any discipline provides possibilities for support, processing of information and experiences, and intellectual and spiritual encounters in a safe environment. Courses that focus on personal spiritual formation or spiritual practices, such as prayer, may be particularly conducive to the development of emotional memory contingent upon any prior connections group members may have with one another or the depth of personal sharing in the groups.

4. Find your core message and repeat it with increasing depth

A core message is the main purpose of an overall class session stripped down to its most critical essence.[17] The core message of your class session should be no longer than one sentence, with seven words maximum. Remember from our earlier discussion of short-term memory that there is a seven-item maximum capacity in this temporary form of memory, although some believe it may be as few as five or six. Creating a core message for each class session not only helps your students remember, but helps you stay focused on a clear goal. Finding the core message in any endeavor is challenging, but particularly so in a context of higher education, where words are the primary currency of communication. It requires professors and lecturers to identify clearly a goal for the learning event and then be able to set aside unrelated but equally valid and important goals for future class sessions. As experts in assessing sticky ideas, Chip and Dan Heath claim that the original sticky idea is the proverb.[18] These pithy nuggets of wisdom have persisted through time. *Don't put all your eggs . . .* , for example. Proverbs are simple yet profound. They are compact yet contain worthwhile information. Think of the core message as a

16. David Hogue, *Remembering the Future, Imagining the Past: Story, Ritual, and the Human Brain* (Cleveland: Pilgrim, 2003).
17. Chip Heath and Dan Heath, *Made to Stick* (New York: Random House, 2007), 28.
18. Ibid., 11.

visual proverb. There is more to a core message than simply being brief. It must be thick, relevant, valuable, and multilayered so that it is not easily dismissed. It must set us on a path of discovery and ignite our curiosity to learn more. Once you have a core message, you need to magnify its stickiness by making it visual. Is there an image that best communicates the core message, but does not detract from the message? You might choose to project this image on a screen, upload it to a LMS, or simply describe the related image verbally, but knowing that vision trumps the other senses, it will be more effective for enhancing memory if it is actually visible to the students.

The cover of the Heaths' *Made to Stick* illustrates an image that clearly communicates their core message.[19]

If you have to hunt for the core message, your brain is working too hard and will likely miss a great deal of information as it seeks the gist. Rather than make your students search for your core message, why not tell them your main goal up front and allow them to use that information as hooks for the remainder of your presentation? Miguel de Cervantes wrote several proverbs, along with his many other literary works. He is said to have defined a proverb as a short sentence drawn from long experience.[20] Conduct your own informal experiment. Use your long experience as a teacher to craft a core message for your next class. Distribute sticky notes to each student at the end of class and ask them to write down the core message they are taking away from class, using no more than seven words. See how closely their take-aways match your intended goal.

Marketing experts and neuroscientists agree that one of the keys to memory is to repeat ideas and concepts with increasing depth. The postmodern curriculum theorist William Doll calls this "recursion."[21] There are two elements to recursive learning: repeating and remembering, which are intertwined and form a continual loop of learning. John Medina's Brain Rules #5 and #6 reinforce the concept of a loop of learning. Medina says that if you want something to stick in short-term memory, you need to repeat to remember; for information and experiences to move from short-term to long-term memory, you need to remember to repeat.[22] Imagine a slinky stretched out with the core idea of your class session at one end. The coils in the slinky represent your lecture, along with other methods you use to help your students engage with the new information, symbolizing the repeated delivery of material that grows in complexity. In recursive learning, the teacher seeks to illustrate, restate, reframe, reinterpret, and return to the core message throughout the

19. QR code URL: http://heathbrothers.com/books/made-to-stick/.
20. Heath and Heath, *Made to Stick*, 17.
21. William E. Doll, "The Four R's—an Alternative to the Tyler Rationale," in *The Curriculum Studies Reader*, 2d ed. (New York: RoutledgeFalmer, 2004), 255–56.
22. Medina, *Brain Rules*, 97–147.

entire class, using a variety of methods and means to broaden and deepen students' understanding. You may wish to revisit Bloom's taxonomy or look at Edgar Dale's Cone of Experience to help create recursive experiences.

Most of us are tempted to impart too much information. Recursive learning is not an opportunity to pack more information into a lecture or simply to restate your last point using different words. The point of recursive learning is not necessarily to allow you to communicate more information but to communicate less information more deeply. Recursive learning is like adding flour to gravy; it must be done slowly and carefully. If teachers verbally overload a lecture or presentation and then immediately repeat it using a similar style or approach, students are likely to tune out and the information is not likely to stick.

Repetition is not simply the tool of the teacher. Students need to be provided with intentional opportunities to rehearse information or concepts in ever-deepening ways and to understand the value of repetition for their own learning. I taught my children how to tie their shoes using the well-known "Bunny Ears" rhyme about a bunny circling around a tree, jumping into a hole, and coming out the other side. As they grew older, they no longer needed to recite the rhyme in order to know how to tie their shoes because they had repeated the process so frequently that it had become part of their motor memory; putting on their shoe triggered the memory. As you make assignments, be aware of repetition and recursion. Repeating a thought process, action, or information produces stronger and more efficient synapses that are less likely to be pruned. The culmination of the ordination exams I took was an extensive New Testament exegesis project. Since I do not regularly use biblical languages, I began brushing up on my Koiné several months before the exam with online flash cards. I was pleasantly surprised to find that after over thirty years I remembered many words and their meanings. In addition, I participated in a weekly Greek New Testament reading group, which allowed me to deepen my memory.

Good teaching will live in the always-shifting working memory of students. Sticky teaching lives in long-term memory by grabbing students' attention (seven-word core message) and by providing opportunities for students to rehearse information (repeat to remember: remember to repeat).

Make It Stick

Practice finding core messages in familiar things. Begin by being particularly attentive to any form of advertising. Immediately after you notice an ad, see if you can identify the advertisers' core message and how it is repeated both visually and verbally. Next, practice finding core messages in sermons. Before you leave a worship service, identify the core message and write it down. Remember, the core message should permeate the entire worship service and be repeated through various means. The sermon is only one communication tool. Finally, practice finding core messages in lectures, either your own or other lectures you attend. As you progress to more and more verbal events, do you notice any differences in the core messages or in your ability to identify them?

5. Demonstrate relevance and create interest; employ the ten-minute rule

We already know several factors that help the brain engage and learn. Neuroscientists and their conversation partners tell us that if information is not connected to prior knowledge, emotionally wired and visually stimulating, we have approximately ninety seconds before the information disappears. It is also true that if your brain cannot make a connection or establish relevance, it determines the information unnecessary and disregards or, worse yet, discards it. If you have a morning class, you need to know that your students come with more attentional neurotransmitters than if your class takes place in the afternoon.[23] That means you need to work harder to capture and keep students' attention after lunch and it gets harder with each passing hour. The longer we focus our attention on an experience, regardless of where or when it occurs, the more likely it is that it will become part of our long-term memory. But this has its limits, too. Neuroscience has also documented a disturbing fact for most professors, preachers, and workshop leaders. Listeners check out of a primarily verbal presentation after about ten minutes. Our task as practitioners of sticky learning is to demonstrate relevance, create interest, and keep our students engaged.

The good news is that there is evidence to suggest effective ways to capture and hold the attention of your listeners, to help them establish the relevance of information and to create interest. If you establish relevance by connecting new information to prior knowledge and create interest by the use of narratives or creating emotion-rich events, how do you sustain interest long enough for the brain to activate long-term storage mechanisms? The way to make long-term memory more reliable is to incorporate new information gradually (tip #4, above) and repeat it in timed intervals of no more than ten minutes.[24] John Medina calls this ten-minute-interval a "hook."

Here are some principles of hooks:

- *Hooks must trigger an emotion.* Narratives are an excellent tool to use, as described in tip #3, if they are short and reinforce the core message. Visual images, as described in tip #1, are also effective.

- *Hooks must be relevant.* This is not the time for a story for story's sake. Telling any old joke is not an effective hook. Listeners will begin to distrust your motives and disconnect; you lose your credibility as a source. Disorganization frustrates the brain and tells it to work harder at creating order. The energy used on creating order from a disjointed presentation takes away from energy that could be used to make a memory.

- *Hooks can serve as transitions.* Review and summarize material or repeat some material in the form of a story or illustration. Ask your

---

23. Marilee Sprenger, *Learning and Memory: The Brain in Action* (Alexandria, VA: Association for Supervision and Curriculum Development, 1999), 95.
24. Medina, *Brain Rules*, 89–93.

students a personally connecting question that either summarizes the immediately previous points or anticipates the upcoming points to allow them to predict where you are heading. Anticipate the next point, ask a surprising and unexpected question, or generate curiosity by finding the gaps in your students' knowledge; all these are effective transitional hooks.

Hooks can and, I believe, should be fun. They should catch us off guard and cause students to look up from their notes. Hooks are not only relevant for your classroom. Your students also need to understand how to craft an effective hook and the role of hooks in engaging the attention of listeners regardless of whether they will pursue a pulpit or Ph.D. In a neurobiological way, we all have some attention deficits. From the lab to the classroom, experts observe that we do not pay attention to things that are boring because our brains are wired to pay attention to things that surprise us, intrigue us, tickle our synapses with novelty, or draw our interest as a prehistoric survival technique. While we no longer have to be aware of wild prey, the basic premise still remains. Our brains pay attention to things that are interesting.

Hooks and the ten-minute rule are one way to capture the attention of our students. Attention is not only maintaining focus for a period of time; attention is also about inhibiting extraneous information, minimizing distractions, and the ability to shift attention between relevant and engaging activities. Attention functions to assist the working memory to stabilize the incoming information and increases the potential for long-term memory. Keeping students' attention can also employ a variety of pedagogical tools. One such tool for short-term memory is "chunking." Chunking works primarily with semantic, or word-based, memory and allows students opportunity to process information in small bits. Chunking functions in the brain to create word-objects as students associate information into groups. The more often we engage in chunking, the more stable the information becomes, thus enabling greater recall. Employed with the ten-minute rule, chunking suggests that a speaker stops presenting information at intervals and facilitates the students' interaction with information. In most cases, that means we ask for questions and when there are none, we proceed with our presentation. That is not chunking! Why? Because there is no interaction with the material if there are no questions. You might consider instead asking students to summarize, paraphrase, or interpret what they just heard, engage in debates on differing points of view, create timelines or grids, or, in limited situations, create real-life role-play situations that apply what they just learned. Chunking implies that the instructor will direct the breaks and design options for students to interact with one another about the material so that they may organize it for themselves. Once again, teaching students how to chunk material outside the classroom supports their long-term memory. This concept may be particularly helpful in disciplines that require memorization, such as church history or biblical languages. Remind students to look for ways to group similar items in categories and to work with material in chunks of five to seven units for most effective recall of information.

"Scaffolding" is not a new concept. It is most often attributed to Lev Vygotsky and his Zone of Proximal Development (ZDP), although he never used the term. Scaffolding education builds a bridge to enable students to arrive at new insights or new knowledge through a process of integration and interaction with either peers or teachers who are more knowledgeable. Scaffolds can be tangible means of organizing material such as syllabi, schemas, graphic organizers, or grids. As a leading learner with your students, you can begin to build a culture of scaffolding by establishing an expectation that all members of a class are both learners and teachers. Openly inviting students to share how and what they have learned from one another enhances that culture. A great deal of work has been done on incorporating scaffolding structures into children's education, but much more thought needs to take place on the role scaffolding might play in education with diverse adult students.

Teachers need to monitor student understanding in order to ensure that students are attentive and engaged. This can be accomplished through interactive activities following a chunked presentation; however, it is important to involve as many students as possible. Based on feedback from student interaction, teachers can adjust the pace of a lecture or presentation or review information that is misunderstood or unclear. The bottom line for keeping the attention of your students is that you must be attentive to the students and their learning process. Creating relevance and interest for your students is a recursive process in many ways. As you employ hooks, emotion, story, chunking, scaffolding, monitoring, and other resources to create engaging learning events that hold the attention of your students, you are guiding them toward deeper and richer ways of knowing.

Make It Stick

Knowing that most instructors are not likely to completely abandon lectures, here are some possible shifts that could turn an ordinary lecture into to a sticky lecture.

- *Don't be boring!* We know that we are less attentive to boring things, so don't be boring and predictable in your lectures. Predictability destroys interest. Use a different device periodically to arouse interest. Experiment with utilizing different senses. Be aware of overusing emotion. Balance is the key; you also want to avoid being so unpredictable that your students become uncomfortable and anxious.

- *Change the pace!*[25] Unbeknownst to us, our students enter the classroom asking two questions in order to assess the importance of what they are about to do. Does this get my attention? Am I emotionally attached to this? In order to get their attention, change the pace of your lecture by:

  – Using a video clip.

---

25. Barbara Bruce, *Our Spiritual Brain* (Nashville: Abington, 2002), 40, 117.

- Taking a straw poll vote on a controversial idea and inviting students to stand in agreement or disagreement then articulate their reasons.

- Using silence. Ask them to take time to write or draw the main ideas they have heard so far. Using an odd number of seconds as an additional surprise element.

- Inviting them to "turn and talk" in groups of two or three; another opportunity to use an odd amount of time for novelty.

- Standing up to do the "turn and talk" exercise.

- Applying biblical-language skills in a "sword-drill" approach. Begin with Bibles closed. Open up to a random location and ask students to identify as many words as they can in a few seconds. You might also provide them with a specific text and invite them to translate spontaneously. I guarantee this will generate some emotional arousal.

- Inviting students to correlate a life experience with a concept.

- Teaching from a different location or position than is customary.

- Beginning a class with various forms of prayer. Inviting students to facilitate class prayer provides even more variety.

• *1+ 9!* If you can state your core message (tip #4) in one minute or less, then spend the next nine minutes describing it, illustrating it, explaining it, and helping others to experience it. Then stop and check in with your students to help them process it. Make your lecture part of the recursive process.

• *Prime the pump!* Prime your students with what you will share with them in one word, a core message, an image, or a clear idea of where you will lead them. "In the next ten minutes, I will be sharing the four key factors in the decline of the prophets . . ." Identify a chunk-word that connects the key points of your lecture and give that word to your students either verbally or visually. Posting lecture notes on the LMS ahead of class can also serve as a primer.

• *Hit the pause button!* If you use video content, consider stopping at a convenient point, no longer than ten minutes, so that students can digest the information. This holds true for guest speakers or demonstrations as well.

• *Close the loop!* It is always a good idea to begin a class by reviewing the previous class material, but remember to close the loop by summarizing what has been covered in today's class. It's even more effective if the students close the loop with your help.

• *Attract attention!* We cannot demand our students' attention. We must attract it. Our brains are designed to be keenly aware of change so the occasional use of creative interruptions, although somewhat risky, can help attract attention. Think about what happens when a car alarm goes off in the middle of your class or someone suddenly drops a book. Creative interruptions are intentional interruptions that you craft to awaken interest. Use any of the ideas in the "Change the pace" section above or create your own interruption. Whatever creative interruptions you choose to employ, remember that you want first and foremost to attract your students into the joy of learning. In addition, the first few minutes of your lecture must capture the attention of your students, so consider carefully how you craft a compelling introduction to use this window of attention-grabbing opportunity.

- *Repeat after me!* Repetition is not simply saying the same thing over. One way to repeat concepts in an ever-deepening approach is to associate it immediately with a real-world example, then ask the students to provide a second illustration. If you made an important point at the beginning of your lecture, repeat it at the end to promote short-term memory. Invite students to look for examples or opportunities to apply lecture concepts in the real world, and then begin the next class session by sharing their examples to support long-term memory.

- *Make it matter!* It's not enough merely to know the point of a lecture. Save your students some time and brain energy by telling them up front why today's information is important and why it matters. Make those initial connections with previous classes or even tell a brief personal story about why this matters to you.

- *Close the windows!* While our computers can easily accommodate multiple application windows at one time, our brains cannot. It simply is not true that we can do two things at one time, especially if both things require our attention. Like the computer, when our brains attempt to multitask and flip between activities that demand our attention, we are time-sharing with decreased effectiveness. Resist encouraging your students to multitask by using documents on your LMS or pointing them to additional online sources during your lecture. Resist posting an outline of the lecture online, then using presentation software in class. If a lecture is based on and will follow closely the content of a digital slideshow or presentation software, then make it easier on your students' brains by posting the exact same presentation on the LMS. By explaining where your lecture is headed at the outset, periodically providing linkages, and staying with concepts consistent with the presentation, your students will be saved from simultaneously struggling to figure out how a concept fits while trying to maintain attention on the lecture.

- *Push back from the podium!* In order to avoid overstuffing ourselves at a holiday dinner, we remind ourselves to push back from the table and to stop when we feel full. This is a reminder to not overstuff your lectures with information overload. Overstuffing, or "info-lust," as one professor dubbed it, only reduces the ability of working memory to function effectively.

- *Act it out!* As you bring your class session to a close, look for ways students may enact what they have learned. Guide your students to imagine they are enacting something you have described, suggested, or explored together. Invite them to suggest scenarios where information may be useful or applicable. If the class content does not suggest particular actions or ways to live out the core message, consider creating some way for learners to reflect, imagine, create, even share ways in which they might embody what they have learned this week in their lives or in their ministry context. This is best done either within the context of the class or very shortly thereafter. Individuals who create a visual picture of themselves acting out something they have learned are more likely to remember and connect the learning with other elements of their lives.

Theological and religious-studies education is about more than information; it encompasses transformation as well. We spend a great deal of time and institutional resources on the informational aspects and less time on evaluating what makes for transformational education. Among many ways to understand transformation, neuroscience offers one way that makes sense for our purposes. Dr. Eric Kandel's sea slugs provide helpful insight on the concept of transformation; when the nervous system changes, there are often correlated changes in behavior. When we observe changes in the way learners respond to situations in life as well as in the classroom, we often identify these behavioral changes as learning, memory, development, or growth. If we observe changes in behavior or actions, we can also surmise that there has been some change in the circuitry of the brain that has prompted the behavioral adaptations. An individual's experiences, both inside and outside of the classroom, are one of the greatest factors affecting our brain's plasticity. Memory cannot be looked at in isolation from behavior. Memory is cemented through action as the motor system enacts what our brain has learned. The motor system is the final pathway of all sensory systems. Kandel makes a bold claim that there is no point in having a thinking process if it cannot be expressed through action.

Until students have an opportunity to live out what they have learned, the learning is not completely cemented in the brain. Any direction for application and action must be authentic and genuine but the relevant information must have been deemed valuable and important to be remembered when the appropriate time comes for action. Memory leads to expression through action—that's transformational education. Transformational education assumes that our lifestyles, choices, responses, thoughts, and reflections are not separate from content and information. It is testing what we have learned in a classroom setting in the context of real life that challenges our knowing and fully integrates the reforming and reshaping not only of our brain, but of our entire being. Transformation of this nature can begin by creating learning experiences that are sticky.

Chapter 6

The Artistic and Even Risky Endeavor of Teaching
A Narrative Response to "Tips for Sticky Learning"

Rodger Y. Nishioka

> "Toto, I've a feeling we're not in Kansas anymore."
> —Dorothy, *The Wizard of Oz*

I so appreciate my colleague and friend, Holly Inglis, and her fine work in helping us all better understand and grasp sticky learning, particularly through her thoughtful examination of what we are coming to know about the brain and how neuroscience is helping us develop a deeper understanding of how we learn. As she does in her first chapter, Holly opens her final chapter using the iconic 1939 American film, *The Wizard of Oz*. She reminds us that, at significant moments in the film, those on the journey had more than one choice before them. As Holly tells us, there were other paths and other roads. The Yellow Brick Road was not the only road available. The same is true for we who are called to teach in these days. When it comes to teaching and learning, there are numerous roads and paths before us. The choices alone are complex, but no matter which road or path we choose, we cannot make one choice: to choose not to make a choice. Upon emerging from her tornado-carried home and seeing the new world in which she has landed, Dorothy makes a claim that is both crucial and obvious even to the casual observer. "Toto," she says to her dog, "I've a feeling we're not in Kansas anymore."

This is true for us all. When it comes to the artistic and even risky endeavor of teaching in the hopes that our students learn and that we as instructors grow with them, this much is true: we are not where we have been. The landscape has changed. There are paths available to us that we had not anticipated or even

---

*QR code URL: https://www.youtube.com/watch?v=vQLNS3HWfCM.

imagined. What, then, are we to do? Holly's final chapter helps us all by clearly identifying "Five tips for sticky learning/sticky teaching." I am drawn not only to the clarity and practicality of these five tips but also to the ways they reflect the theoretical and conceptual foundations Holly has so thoughtfully put before us. In this response, I will add my own observations about these five tips in hopes that my own experiences and reflections might add another dimension to Holly's good work. Like Dorothy, who sought companions on the journey (which is, by the way, always a wise thing to do, especially when confronting an unfamiliar landscape), I am privileged to join Holly and you, the reader, as together we choose a path and discover what adventures, sustained by the grace of God, await us all.

It Started with a Raisin

Holly's first tip for sticky learning and sticky teaching calls us to stimulate more senses in our teaching so that our students better grasp and retain the learning. I was teaching an introductory doctoral seminar for students in our Christian spirituality concentration and my faculty colleague, Barbara Brown Taylor, was a guest lecturer that day. Her primary invitation was to engage us in recalling how we yearn for the Holy Spirit. We started by reading Psalm 63 out loud together ("O God, you are my God. I seek you, my soul thirsts for you; my flesh faints for you, as in a dry and weary land where there is no water"). Then Barbara moved around the classroom and gave each one of us a raisin. She then invited us to put the raisin in our mouths and to note its texture and taste and to hold the raisin on our tongues. Then she read the psalm again and ended in silence, inviting us to give attention to what was happening to the raisin. As Barbara read and then, as we were silent, the raisin that had started out as a hard, bumpy, small morsel began to change. I was surprised by how quickly this happened. The raisin, drawing from the moisture of my saliva, began to grow plump and full. As far as I could tell, it more than quadrupled in size. Eventually, it felt smooth on my tongue. After a few moments, Barbara invited us to bite into it, and its sweetness squirted into my mouth. Each of us savored that raisin and held it before swallowing. Then she read the psalm again and invited us to reflect out loud on what it means first to be dry and parched and then to yearn and thirst for God and finally to encounter God as a wellspring that parches our thirst and satisfies our longing.

Later, over lunch, I remember the animated conversation at tables as we talked about that experience of the raisin and how the words of the psalm writer became so real to us. One student, a pastor in a congregation in North Carolina, told us that his routine was to have a bowl of raisin bran every morning for breakfast. A creature of habit, he had done this for years, much to the chagrin of his wife and children. "In all these years," he said, "I never paid attention to what happened to the raisins, probably because I was scanning the newspaper online or catching up on the plans for the day and caught in the activity around me. I will never look at or eat those raisins in the same way. Every time I have breakfast, I will reflect on the words from Psalm 63. Better yet, when I get home I am going to read the psalm to my wife and kids while they have a raisin in their mouths." We enjoyed the image of that family gathered around the breakfast table in the midst of the hustle and bustle of a school morning and our friend trying to get them to be attentive to the words of the psalmist. Several of us encouraged him to think about another, better time, perhaps an evening devotion, but, nevertheless, to share this experience with them and, more importantly, to tell them how meaningful this was to their husband and dad. That's what is so wonderful about sticky learning. When learning sticks, we know it and, not only that, we yearn to share it with others, not so that the experience can be replicated but so that this knowing, this transformation, may be mutually shared and expanded.

At Columbia Theological Seminary where I teach, we gather four times a week for community worship. Just like at many seminaries and theological schools, worship is planned and led by professors, staff colleagues, students, alumni, administrators, local pastors, visiting scholars, and any combination of those just listed. On Friday, we share in the Lord's Supper together. To be honest, while we have a variety of denominations and liturgical traditions in our community, most times the communion liturgy is pretty standard. We are fortunate to have two professors who teach in the area of worship. On one Friday, one of the worship professors, Kim Long, was presiding at the table; she had just led her class on worship and the sacraments through a variety of experiences in celebrating the sacrament of the Lord's Supper. In one of these, she challenged the class to give more attention to what persons in the congregation see rather than what they hear. So, after saying the prayer over the bread and the wine, and including the traditional words of institution in the prayer ("We give thanks to you, O God, that when he was at supper with his disciples, Jesus took bread and blessed it and broke it and gave it to them . . ."), she looked up at the congregation with a broad smile, purposefully lifted up the bread and, without saying words, she broke it over her head; then, gesturing to us all with halves of the now-divided loaf in each hand, in a broad, sweeping, and expansive motion she demonstrated how this was now given for us. Then she put the bread down, lifted up the cup and pitcher, poured the wine from the pitcher into the chalice, and, in a similar way, gestured with the cup in a broad, sweeping, and expansive motion. She then set the pitcher down and took a half of the loaf of bread in her hand and, keeping the cup in the other, walked out from behind the communion table into the aisles of the chapel, moving and gesturing to persons, showing us how the bread and wine were given to us and for us, all without speaking a single word. She returned to the table and invited the servers to come forward and then gestured to us all, again without one word being said, and, as we were able, we rose and moved to the table to partake of the generous meal set before us.

When Holly reminds us that, of all the senses, vision engages the most of our brainpower, that illustration of Professor Long at the table comes immediately to mind. Do not get me wrong. I am not dismissing our words. Indeed, we who teach know of the importance of language and, in the twenty-first century in particular, language matters as it has the power to create what we come to know and believe as reality. Yet, it is equally true that our attention is captured best by what we see. In conversations with many young people, when they talk about being "bored" in the classroom or in worship, what they actually are saying is that they, more than any other generation, are visual. They need to see it to know it. Again, this does not preclude or dismiss the value of language used for reflection and for testing what one sees, because any of our senses can deceive us. But it is important that, as teachers, we recognize that many of our learners are yearning to *see* something first and then to discuss it and reflect upon it.

In recent years, I have become a collector of sets of images printed on heavy cardstock. It amazes me how often I may use the same sets of images in different ways throughout a semester. Placing the same set of images on tables around the classroom, I may invite students to choose an image that most closely represents their image of the Holy Spirit before launching into a study of pneumatology. A few class sessions later, I will put out the same set of images and invite students to choose an image that speaks to them of ministry in the twenty-first century as we prepare to hear from a panel of current pastors, church educators, and youth-ministry leaders. In every situation, I am asking the learner to engage the visual sense to prepare us to be attentive to the topic of the day. Even at the end of the term, I will hear students remark about seeing an image for the "first time." In other cases, one student will choose the same image but, through their imagination, see something completely different, given the task at hand. Always, I am impressed by how the energy in the learning space rises as students discuss the image and its meaning for them and for us all. This very simple way of engaging their brains and focusing their attention takes all of five minutes but, at the end of that time, they are more attentive and more present because of they have been invited to open their minds and see.

May the Lord Bless You and Keep You . . .

Toni is a gift to any classroom. She is a natural synthesizer. She makes connections. It's in her very nature. It is how her brain is wired. Sometimes, the connections may seem a little convoluted, but I and her peers have learned to stay with her to see where she ends up. This in itself can be great fun. She is one of those who freely admits that for her to "get it," she needs to talk it out. At one point, I asked the class if this was okay, and Josh said that at first it used to annoy him but now he realizes it helps him make connections, too. Toni smiled at that and said "Thank you" to Josh. He smiled back and said, "Go for it, Toni," and so she did.

Holly reminds us that good instructors know that our students, by and large, bring prior knowledge with them to any learning situation. Sometimes, that learning is a problem because it may need to be disputed and significantly revised but, nevertheless, it is prior knowledge and any good teacher must do more than acknowledge this—they must embrace it. For me, in addition to the classroom assessment techniques that Holly highlighted, it is the relatively simple task of inviting students to ponder a question around the topic for the day ("Think about a time when you felt closest to God"). After a few moments of thinking time, I will invite persons to turn to a neighbor or two and share what they were think-ing. Then, after three or four minutes, I will call everyone back to the whole group and move to the teaching for the day or draw out some of their experiences. As a teacher of teaching, I will often stop the class and draw the students' attention to my pedagogy and invite reflection upon that. Even if students may feel inadequate about the topic of the day, these are *students* and every one of them has experienced educative pedagogy and miseducative pedagogy. They have clear prior knowledge about when they knew they were learning and when they knew they were not. My greatest worry and concern is when students come to my class having experienced such silencing, that they discount that prior knowledge.

Esther joined us as an exchange student from a seminary in South Korea. She was with us for one year and struggled mightily with the American classroom and learning style. Coming from a more formal schooling system, she was perplexed by the informal rules for interaction. Several times in my class, I caught her simply staring at another student wide-eyed, almost disbelieving that the student was raising questions with me about my teaching (something that I have come to love, by the way, although in my early, more insecure years, I did not handle this as well). She made an appointment and came to my office, in and of itself a courageous act, and as soon as she was in my office, apologized for taking up my time. When I assured her I was glad to see her and thanked her for *her* time, she appeared befuddled, not sure if I was being serious. After several minutes of discussion about readings and assignments, she asked about my own background as an Asian American and wondered how I felt in the classroom. I told her some of my own history and that, as a fourth-generation Japanese American, I was clearly straddling the line between my Japanese heritage and my American identity. Then we got to the heart of the matter. She wondered why I invited so much discussion in the classroom and worried that when I called on her and she did not answer, that I would think she had not prepared. I assured her that I knew she was prepared because I had seen her studying in the library and, while moving around the classroom, I had glanced at her textbooks that were marked up with different colors and translations in the margins. She seemed relieved at this. When I asked her why she did not answer when I invited her to speak in class, she told me it was because it was not "her place" to answer. Then she began to explain that in her school in South Korea, she is one of a few women and is often assigned by the almost-always male professor or instructor to sit in the back of the class. In most classes, students are never called upon, but in the few classes where they are, the professor always calls on the men and never the women. I asked her if she thought this was right and then quickly realized the question in and of itself was not only absurd to her, but even beyond her consideration as one who has been nurtured and formed in an authoritarian, patriarchal, and hierarchical culture.

Holly's second valuable tip for learning to stick is that we as teachers draw upon the student's prior knowledge. For Esther, even though she surely had such knowledge, having spent her whole life in the church (she was the daughter of a pastor father and church-musician mother, both of whom strongly encouraged her to go to seminary and support the full inclusion of women in church leadership), the academy had taught her that her prior knowledge was not worthy. Esther was in class with me for both semesters of her year-long study, and I told her that part of her work with us here was to help her know that her prior knowledge is worthy of being shared with others and that, in this sharing, it helps not only her learning but all of us. I told her my task was to help bring her to voice (to use the marvelous feminist/womanist language) and asked if that was something she would like to explore further with me and others. Hesitant at first, she eventually agreed.

By the close of the last semester of her time with us, Esther was freely making connections. In fact, in one marvelous exchange, after Toni, who was in the this same class, made connections about the learning to her own African American church experiences, Esther spoke up (without raising her hand?!) and made connections to her own South Korean church experience. After she had shared, Toni told her how helpful that was; the class spontaneously broke out into applause and Esther beamed.

Good teachers know that their students bring prior knowledge. Further, good teachers know how to bring students to voice so that connections may be made between new learning and that prior knowledge. Esther made one final office appointment with me before leaving for home. True to our shared Asian heritage, she brought a gift to me as a thank-you. She was startled when I gave a gift to her, a votive candle holder placed in a pewter circle engraved with the blessing from Numbers 6:24. After we prayed together, I smiled and spoke the words to Esther. "May the Lord bless you and keep you. May the Lord make his face to shine upon you and be gracious to you. May the Lord lift up his countenance upon you, and give you peace for all of your days." Teary, Esther said she was not sure how she would fare back at her home seminary. I told her I thought she would do well. "But it will be so hard to return to my old ways," she explained. "You are not returning to your old ways," I assured her. "You know now that you bring with you into any classroom not simply the capacity to learn but learning that is already inside of you and worthy of sharing." "I hope so," she said. "I know it," I told her. "How do you know it?" asked Esther. "How can you be so sure?" "I know it," I told her, "because I have seen it."

Welcome to Home . . .

I was thrilled. I was preaching and speaking at Old First Presbyterian Church in the heart of San Francisco. Saturday night, the young-adult group was taking me out to dinner. San Francisco is the one of the world's great eating cities and while I am no "foodie," I know good food when it is put before me, so I was looking forward to the dinner with these young adults. You can imagine my surprise, then, when they picked me up at my hotel and we walked a few blocks into the Tenderloin district, up to a restaurant whose moniker was "Home." There was a line out the door. The group assured me this was a "hot" restaurant and had received rave reviews. They did not take reservations and because it was Saturday night and we were a large group of seventeen, we waited for over an hour and a half for a table. Although the conversation was great while we were waiting, I was hungry when we finally were seated and then was disappointed when I opened my menu to discover that "Home" served things like meatloaf and mashed potatoes, turkey and dressing, chicken-and-rice casserole, and macaroni and cheese. And of course, since it was San Francisco, this was $34 macaroni and cheese. I could not believe it. The young adults were oooohhhing and aaaaahing over the menu and, when the food came, they devoured it, remarking how it reminded them of their grandparents' cooking. Said Devon seated across from me, "Hey . . . welcome to home."

So, I thought about that experience in San Francisco when I read Holly's third tip about sticky learning, that emotional memory trumps all other forms of memory. These hip, bright, thoughtful young adults shared an emotional connection to this food. Even if they had never experienced this food themselves growing up (one of them told me she never knew her grandparents and all her own parents did for meals was order take-out), they yearned for that emotional connection. They were creating that emotional memory and, while I would have preferred something else, they were being genuine and real and welcoming me into that same shared emotional memory—welcoming me into their ideal of home.

Good preachers know and value this emotional connection. They know that as fine as their exegetical skills may be, the sermon, to truly communicate and be *remembered*, must offer an emotional connection—some call it a hook—every few minutes. The same is true in the classroom. Emotional connections to the learning help us remember.

April 16, 2007, was a Monday, and I was teaching a class on young-adult ministry. We were talking about the sociocultural development issues facing young adults when a student from another class stepped in and, apologizing for interrupting, asked if we had heard that there was a shooting happening on the campus of Virginia Tech University. We had not; she said she was not sure about the details but that her home church was in Blacksburg and she knew a lot of faculty, students, and staff who worshiped there, and asked us to pray. Right away, several of the students went online and we listened as different students relayed the horrible news. By the end of that tragic day, thirty-two students and faculty had been shot and killed, the shooter himself had taken his own life, and seventeen others were wounded. That we were just talking about young adults and that one of our students knew that university and town well, it just all seemed too much to bear. I asked the students to pray with me and then, because I was overwhelmed by the fact that these students and faculty and staff were just like us, simply trying to go to school, I began to cry. It took me some time before I could get any words out. Other students began to cry, too, and we just sat in silence with some of us, at intermittent moments, voicing a prayer, reading Scripture, or singing a song. I remember after a while, I ended the class and went to my office and wept.

A little over a month later, we were at the reception after our commencement ceremony and Sarah, who was in that young-adult ministry class and had just graduated, came over with her parents to introduce us. I love these moments when I get to meet the family of those whom I have come to know over their years of study. The father and mother were kind, and I shared words with them of how much I loved Sarah and was privileged to be with her in her studies. The father stopped me in midsentence and told me he wanted to thank me for making such a deep impression on her. I smiled and said that was very gracious, but then he interrupted me again and more forcefully looked me in the eyes and said he wanted to make sure I understood. And with Sarah then standing next to me arm in arm, her father explained how Sarah had called and told them about my reaction to the horrible shooting at Virginia Tech. He told me that my reaction had left an indelible impression on her. I was becoming embarrassed, but then Sarah spoke up and said to me, "I told them what amazed me about you, Rodger. I realized that you didn't even know these people, but yet, you loved them and you were heartbroken, even for the young man who shot these people. You truly loved them. I could feel it. I learned a lot from you in your classes," she said. "But I will remember that forever. And I am praying that God helps me do the same always."

In that class, we covered the whole landscape about young adults. Who they are. What they are seeking. We read and talked about them spiritually, theologically, developmentally, and ecclesially. And Sarah was kind to say she learned a lot (although with Sarah I believe that to be true, whereas I am not always so sure when other students say it). But it was telling to me that what she remembered the most was the honest emotion I showed, and that we all shared, about an incident that was outside of the class curriculum yet, truth be told, very much at the center of it.

Holly is also exactly right to warn us against being emotionally manipulative. This kind of abuse has no place in the classroom, and we must guard against it. But just as we are cautious and careful about the manipulation of emotion, we should not shy away from those moments when genuinely and authentically the Holy Spirit invites our affect to lead our cognition, rather than the other way around, which is so often the result of our training as scholars.

In this more cynical and skeptical age, I think we have become more suspicious and wary of emotion, and perhaps it is right that we do so. While we should not attempt to construct or create emotional moments for our students, because we know that emotion-laden events are retained and remembered, neither should we reject them or neglect them when the emotion is honest, authentic, and true.

Story Linking . . .

It is also of great help that Holly reminds us of the power of story to evoke emotion. Narrative preachers know this and have honed their ability to tell the biblical narrative in such a way that persons remember and are even welcomed in to the story. But again, wary of emotional manipulation, this is not story for the sake of emotional engagement. Good teachers know that the power of story is not to be taken lightly. Stories must be relevant to the topic and, as in good narrative preaching, invite the hearer into the story as a participant who then is able to share their own story. Further, these stories cannot stand alone. They must be in relationship with one another rather than in competition with one another. And always, always, they must join with the grand story of the God's revelation made known to us in Jesus Christ.

Anne Streaty Wimberly, professor emeritus at the Interdenominational Theological Center here in Atlanta, calls this the story-linking process. In her marvelous book, *Soul Stories: African American Christian Education*, she beautifully illustrates the power of the story in the African American church, most often through shared testimony. But the test of this testimony is not how well it reflects upon the storyteller but, rather, in how the testimony links to the ongoing story of the faithful people of God and, in Anne's particular context, the historic African American church witness, and then, further, how well this links to the story of God's faithfulness and revelation.

In a class I teach, titled "Transforming the Confirmation Journey" (in my own tradition, confirmation is a rite of passage for adolescents when they make a public profession of faith in a way that the congregation can affirm, and then the young persons commit themselves to grow as followers of Jesus), we were exploring during one session the importance of the adult mentor—someone who is not the adolescent's parent or guardian but, rather, another faithful adult in the congregation who accompanies the young person throughout his or her confirmation journey—and I shared a story about Jenn and Carly. Carly was Jenn's adult mentor and a Delta flight attendant. During the year-long confirmation journey, Carly faithfully sent Jenn a postcard from wherever she was in the world. After the confirmation journey was over, Jenn and Carly kept in contact, which often happens when this relationship is nurtured and done well. At one point, I was in Jenn's home during a youth event and her Mom asked if I had a moment. Jenn was downstairs in the basement with the other young people and adults. I followed Jenn's mom to Jenn's bedroom and peeked inside. I was startled to see one whole wall filled with postcards—and not the picture side but, rather, the written side. The postcards, easily over two hundred of them, were from Carly during Jenn's confirmation year. Last fall, Jenn left home for her first year of college in Ohio. At church, Jenn's mom told me that when she went into Jenn's room after she had left, she knew something was different and quickly realized all the postcards were gone. A week later, she mentioned to Jenn that it was too bad she had tossed the postcards; Jenn replied that she had not tossed them—she had taken them with her. They were in a card file in her dorm room in chronological order. Surprised, Jenn's mom asked her why she took them with her, to which Jenn replied, "Because they remind me that I belong to God forever." In fact, on the first day of classes, Jenn said, she woke up early and read through them once again to remind herself of who she was.

We had spent the class period working through a curriculum for mentors and talking about their role and how to recruit and support them, but it was in that story about Carly and Jenn that I could see the "aha" happening for many of my students and, no doubt, some of the skeptics were converted. That's what the power of emotion through story does for us. It offers us an epiphany, a new way of knowing and seeing that convicts us to the truth of the gospel.

If You Don't Know Where You're Going . . .

Before God's call to seminary, I taught public school for four years. The school district where I was first hired as a novice middle-school teacher had a marvelous first-year teacher-training program. Our first session was on creating learning objectives and student outcomes and then crafting lesson plans that truly reflected those learning objectives and student outcomes. This might all sound rather pedestrian, but our instructor was engaging and helpful and, for new teachers about to face thirty-plus students, we were anxious and therefore attentive. One of the first things the instructor did was distribute to each of us a poster with the image of a turtle. The aphorism on the poster read: "If you don't know where you're going . . . you're likely to end up there." I put the poster up above my desk at the back of my classroom. Holly's fourth point resonates with that poster. Good teachers know the core message of their teaching session and repeat it, not just with reiteration, but with increasing depth and complexity.

I was teaching a class session on social cognition for a teaching and learning course. The objective for the particular session was for my students to understand what social cognition is and how they can hone their own social cognition, because an essential task of any good teacher is the ability to read what is happening among her students in the learning setting.

To get there, we started off with an activity. As each student was welcomed to the room, I gave them an envelope that contained a note indicating a role to play. There were positive roles (affirm others genuinely and consistently) and neutral roles (inquire of others without being invasive) and negative roles (be sarcastic with a touch of skepticism and cynicism). I then gave the students a sheet with the names of all persons in the class and, over the next few moments, invited them simply to interact with one another, recording what they thought the other student's role was, thereby testing their social cognition. After a few minutes, I called the students together and each person guessed each other's role, which they then confirmed or corrected. I then asked the class to assure one another that they were only playing a role (although, if truth be told, some of the student's roles were remarkably close to the real persona they live out in the community). What followed was a mini-lecture on social cognition and then a discussion of key theorists and how one's skills in social cognition may be honed and refined as a teacher. There was a closing activity that gave students additional practice in their social-cognitive skills. Further, in the next three days students were to post on the online course-learning site five situations when they practiced their social-cognitive skills for all to read and possibly respond. The core message was certainly about social cognition and its importance as a skill for the teacher and, as the session progressed, students were invited more deeply to explore and synthesize the core message.

Holly's words are so important here. This is not simply repetition for regurgitation. The core message is one that stands amidst us all and is held up for increasingly more complex and, consequently, more generative study and reflection. In this way, we move beyond the surface to a deeper and more resonant and enduring knowing.

In recent years, when a student (or students) has struggled with how I have tried to teach the core message, I have turned to others to assist. At one point during this session on social cognition, one student, clearly frustrated, blurted out, "I just don't think I understand what you're trying to get me to know about this social-cognition stuff." In my more immature days, I would have either gotten defensive or tried harder to explain and make the student understand—most likely both. But a few years ago, after realizing doing this just made both of us more frustrated, I turned to the class and asked if anyone could offer to help with further explanation or illustration (not the student who was frustrated). After a few seconds of waiting, a couple of students ventured forth a different explanation and then, space having been made for all of us to share in some way as participants in our knowing and learning and teaching, the conversation began to open up and some other deeper questions surfaced leading us to a greater complexity and depth of knowing. Through these experiences and others, I came to realize the truth of my pedagogical claim that knowing, and therefore sticky learning (as Holly would tell us), is greatly increased when it is socially constructed—that is, when teacher and student alike join together as co-learners and co-constructors of our knowing. This by no means dismisses the inherent power imbalance of the classroom. To make the claim that we are all equals here would be to neglect the very role to which I have been called. But more and more I am convinced that in order to bring clarity and depth to the core message, we instructors have to welcome other voices—not simply other published scholarly voices, but the voices of our student scholars as well.

Keeping It Real

I teach Christian education, which is lodged in the broader academic area of practical theology (hey, come on—that's not an oxymoron!). For that reason, I love Holly's final tip on demonstrating relevance and creating interest and her explanation of the ten-minute rule. This final sticky tip is full of creative and real ways to engage our learners in the new landscape in which we find ourselves as teachers. And because I teach in the field of practical theology, you might think (and you would be wrong) that I never hear the question: "So, why do we have to know this?" or "What does this have to do with my call to ministry?" Here's the challenge about relevance: what is real to one person may not be real to another person and, even for the same person, what may be real at one point in their life may not be real at another point in her or his life. I get it. We are talking about a shifting landscape here. It is not only that Dorothy and Toto are not in Kansas anymore. It is that the land in which they find themselves is itself changing and shifting beneath their feet. Further, if neuroscience is correct, and there is every evidence that it is, the brain itself is changing—rewiring itself—in response to different experiences and stimuli and technologies. This is why in a learning space whose student ages run the gamut from twenty-somethings to seventy-somethings, our task of teaching is even more challenging. But here is the thing: if knowing and learning are socially constructed, then homogeneity is a problem because, by our very lack of difference, our knowing and learning are hindered by our similar experiences and similar worldviews. In contrast, then, heterogeneity, as much of a challenge as it is, is ultimately rewarding and enhances our knowing and learning.

While I love this section and find it very helpful and full of imagination with practical ideas and novel methods, I am reminded ultimately that keeping it real is less about the next creative activity or hook or method and more about the person of the teacher. After all, we teach who we are. In Matthew 6:21, Jesus says "For where your treasure is, there will your heart be also." For me, the pedagogical caveat would be, "For where your treasure is, there will your teaching be also."

Method is important. Hooks are important. Strategies are important. But, ultimately, what we teach is ourselves more than our methods, hooks, and strategies. We are into our second week of Greek school, an intensive language study that some students take during the summer. Our senior New Testament professor here at Columbia is Elizabeth Johnson. She is a skilled and gifted teacher and, while our new students are stressing over vocabulary and Greek participles, she reminds them why they are doing this (her core message and way of keeping it real). By the third day they were reading verses in their Greek Bibles and the excitement was palpable (one of the study groups meets in the classroom across from my office). But the excitement was not simply about being able to read in this ancient language. The excitement was because their instructor who has spent her whole life reading and studying these words actually *loves* them. That's right. She *loves* the Bible. She loves it because she believes with her whole being that somehow, by the grace of God and through God's Holy Spirit, these stories about and words from Jesus Christ reveal to us more and more about who God is and what it means to love God with all our heart, and with all our soul, and with all our mind, and with all our strength, and to love others in God's name. That's where her treasure is. That's where her teaching is also.

The landscape is shifting even at times beneath our very feet. But the call is the same no matter whether we are in Oz or Kansas or Saskatchewan or California. The call is to keep our treasure not in our methods or strategies or even in ourselves. The call is to keep our treasure in the one who created us and redeemed us and sustains us no matter where we are. For where our treasure is so will our heart be . . . so will our teaching be . . . and that, my friends, is keeping it real.

Chapter 7

What's a Teacher to Do?

Holly J. Inglis

With a basic understanding of the nature of learning, how our brain works, how memory develops, and specific tips for sticky learning, our final destination is to consider the changing role of the instructor in a brain-friendly classroom. The concept of "brain-based learning" arose in the 1980s as Leslie Hart, Howard Gardner, and Geoffrey and Renate Caine began to connect cognitive processes with classroom methods and developed new models of thinking about and practicing education. "Brain-based learning" has a myriad of suggestions and approaches, but the overarching theme is that when teachers teach and students learn in accordance with how our brain is designed, the learning is more effective and stands a greater chance of becoming long lasting, memorable, and sticky. A secondary theme in the literature is, at times, cautiously alluded to and, at other times, is boldly stated: education at all levels is in need of reform, not merely from a political or financial viewpoint, but from a pedagogical and structural perspective. This argument sounds a wake-up call for most educators who want to make the greatest impact on their students, but who realize that much of what they do may be mandated by either a spoken or unspoken institutional pedagogical approach and that any changes they implement in an individual classroom, while affecting some students, may not have a dramatic impact on the overall educational philosophy of the institution. It takes courage not only to make changes in your own classroom, but to suggest that your institution might examine the way it approaches curriculum design, the physical structure of its facility and classrooms, how it uses technology, course evaluation, and student assessment in light of brain-based concepts.

---

*QR code URL: http://seminariumblog.org/general/the-changing-understanding-of-how-we-learn-part
-2-what-is-effective-learning/.

Literature has only recently begun to emerge from practitioners in religious and theological education applying the concept of brain-based learning, so most of what informs this discussion comes from educators in other arenas of education. Inasmuch as neuroscientists do not always agree on the interpretation of scientific data, these educators also have varying interpretations of how the neuroscience can and should be applied to teaching. Many are skeptical and worry that in an age of standardized testing and test-driven evaluations of educators, information on learning and memory might be viewed as a means to manipulate the learning environment in order to achieve higher outcomes.

Recognizing how our brains are wired to learn and remember has far greater ramifications for higher education than simply improving test scores. It has the potential to transform countless lives. Neurologist-turned-educator Judy Willis offers concrete suggestions for classrooms at all levels, but also suggests that students who are preparing to become professional teachers should receive foundational knowledge of how the brain learns and be able to understand and employ specific tools that are known to influence learning and the acquisition of long-term memory so that the students whom they will eventually teach will not only learn more and perform better on tests, but be enabled to achieve their highest potentials. But why stop with only educating teachers? If all students are taught about how our brains learn and remember best, and are encouraged to be more conscious of their own learning, they gain not only the content knowledge of the subject but metacognitive skills as well, which can foster lifelong learning and possibly influence a wider audience as well.

Practicing sticky learning in a seminary or religious-studies classroom has the potential not only to stimulate and inspire your students, but contains a larger purpose. What happens in your classroom can influence what happens in congregations, future classrooms, workshops, and other settings as students graduate and begin to teach others as they were taught, replicating not only *what* they learned but *how* they learned. Your ability to affect how your students learn as well as what they learn can have enormous ramifications when you consider how many people will hear the sermons your students preach, attend their workshops, retreats, or classes, or read their books or blogs or articles. If they learn from a teacher who understands brain-based learning and who helps her or his students understand the content of the course as well as how they can most effectively learn and remember, they are much more likely to teach in a brain-based manner as well.

Academics and researchers alike are calling for pedagogical changes. We are at a pedagogical turning point, says Richard Newton, Seminarium blogger and teacher-scholar-student.[1] Israel Galindo, associate dean for Lifelong Learning at Columbia Theological Seminary, author, and frequent contributor to the Wabash Center's blog for theological-school deans, says that we must begin to understand who is

---

1. Richard Newton, "A Call to ACE Critical Reasoning for the Last Time," Seminarium Blog, August 21, 2013, http://seminariumblog.org/general/semclass/newtonr52013/.

doing the most learning in any educational setting.[2] The one who does the most talking, the one who is standing and moving, and the one who is most excited about the ideas and information is most likely to be the one doing the most learning. In most classrooms, the one doing the most learning is the teacher. To alter this picture may feel like a power shift. There is an undeniable element of "letting go" that must accompany a shift from conventional teaching toward sticky learning. This shift is more a continuum of change than an either-or dichotomy. It requires changes for both the teacher and the student in both theory and practice, and language and behavior, but they are changes that can take place intentionally and gradually. Rather than dwelling on the perception of "giving away," consider what you gain by allowing your students to construct their own knowledge in ways that are persistent and transformative. Table 7.1 summarizes the highlights of our journey to the Land of Sticky Learning, focusing on the role and function of the teacher as you to begin to consider how you might begin to enrich your classroom pedagogy.[3]

Throughout my college, seminary, and postgraduate experience, there have been certain teachers who stood out as truly great educators. I usually gave these teachers high marks on course evaluations because I felt I truly learned something in their class, and because they ignited something within me for the subject matter and for my own greater desire to learn. What is it that makes a teacher go from being a good teacher to a great teacher? Ben Johnson, an educational consultant, writes in his Edutopia blog, "Great teachers engineer learning experiences that maneuver the students into the driver's seat and then the teachers get out of the way."[4] Being considered a great teacher may best be described as an act of courageous leadership. In a blog for *Harvard Business Review*, Greg Satell characterizes the primary quality needed in order to engineer change is not authority, but leadership: leadership that empowers and inspires rather than authority that demands and controls.[5] Instead of a medal for courage, like the one presented to the Cowardly Lion by the Wizard, our reward for demonstrating courage is the "velcro" moment: that moment when you know that a learning experience is connecting with your students. Sometimes, even with the most intentional efforts at creating sticky learning, the outcome is still unpredictable, and so the moment when a student lights up with an insight, or a connection, or a new awareness is a memorable one. Perhaps you can recall that kind of transcendent moment in your own experience.

---

2. Israel Galindo, "Everything You Know About Teaching Is Wrong," Columbia Connections Blog, June 13, 2014, http://columbiaconnections.org/2014/06/13/everything-you-know-about-teaching-is-wrong/.

3. Robert B. Barr and John Tagg, "From Teaching to Learning—A New Paradigm for Undergraduate Education," *Change* (November/December 1995): 13–25.

4. Ben Johnson, "Great Teachers Don't Teach," Edutopia blog, June 28, 2013, http://www.edutopia.org/blog/great-teachers-do-not-teach-ben-johnson.

5. Greg Satell, "To Create Change, Leadership Is More Important than Authority," Harvard Business Review Blog, April 21, 2014, http://blogs.hbr.org/2014/04/to-create-change-leadership-is-more-important-than-authority/.

Table 7.1

TEACHING	STICKY LEARNING
Goal of teacher	**Goal of teacher**
Provide instruction and content	Facilitate learning
Transmission of knowledge from teacher	Lead students on journey of discovery
Theory	**Theory**
Knowledge is primarily external	Knowing is internal
Knowledge based on content	Knowing based on integration of experience with content
Knowledge is linear	Knowing is recursive
Knowledge is controlled by teacher	Knowing is dynamic and shared
Teacher is primarily a gatekeeper	Teacher is primarily a curator
Student is primarily passive object of knowledge	Student is primarily active subject of knowing
Classroom experience	**Classroom experience**
Competitive, individualistic	Collaborative, supportive
Frequently unisensory	Frequently multisensory
Teaching concludes when class ends	Learning continues when class ends
Assessment	**Assessment**
Standardized	Metacognition
Primarily content with some application	Primarily integrated application of content
Research-based or short-term memorization	Project- or portfolio-based through integration of experience/passion with information
Methods designed primarily by teacher	Methods may be designed in cooperation between student and teacher
Student outcome	**Student outcome**
Short-term declarative memory (factual information)	Long-term memory
Understanding, storage, and retrieval of information—recall	Understanding, storage, and retrieval has multiple, robust links in the brain—remembering
Application is heavily formalized and is based primarily in objective concepts	Application and transfer through action-reflection-action
Knowledge structures may be expanded but original misconceptions may still exist	Knowledge structures are modified—transformation in approach to new, real-world situations
Learners are primarily externally motivated for short-term success	Learners are primarily internally motivated, which persists beyond the structured class for long-term success
Learners assume and take on the knowledge of the teacher	Learners construct their own knowledge through co-creative problem solving

Want to visualize how to start a movement toward sticky learning in your context? Watch this YouTube video.[6]

James Zull, professor of biology at Case Western Reserve University and *not* a theologian, goes so far as to say that when the unpredictable and mysterious (transcendent) happens in a class, it is like a religious experience. Parker Palmer suggests that good teaching is less of a technique than an act of hospitality. Helping students learn could be imagined as an act of setting the table: creating an inviting, welcoming space where students can bring all of who they are to the task of learning, including their experience, their questions, their emerging ideas that may be different than the professor's, and their previous knowledge. Perhaps teaching could even be viewed as sacramental, an invitation to share in the feast together as co-learners. Students will come from the North, and the South, and the East, and the West to sit at your table. By taking this journey to the Land of Sticky Learning, I hope you are inspired to set a lavish table of rich, multisensory, recursive, emotion-laden, and connected learning experiences for your students as you share in the feast of learning together.

6. QR code URL: http://www.youtube.com/watch?v=s2FzpAFegXE.

Chapter 8

Reimagining Course Design: A Case Study

Kathy L. Dawson

"What is the riskiest thing in your dissertation?" This was a question posed to me at the end of my two-hour dissertation defense at Princeton Theological Seminary in 2002. Having drawn on many of the theorists so eloquently brought to our notice in Holly Inglis's work, what I really wanted to answer was, "I wonder what theological education would look like if we were to take all of this seriously." I figured at that point, however, that the assembled professors and I would be there another two hours or more if I voiced this, so I settled for something less controversial and more personal that could not be disputed. I'm grateful for the opportunity to now show in this chapter some of the beginnings to that never-voiced response.

This chapter uses a pseudo case-study approach to show how the ideas Inglis elaborates upon above are synthesized into course design and planning. For purposes of this project, I have chosen a required basic Christian-education class, but here I talk mainly about process rather than content to open up the discussion to a wider audience. It is divided into three sections—(1) challenges of course design for a basic course (including choice of content and aims); (2) structure of learning (maximizing class times by using learning theory and brain research); (3) and assessment (when long-term memory rather than short-term testing/quizzes/papers are the norm).

Many seminary and religious-studies professors are faced with the task of teaching a basic course in their field of study that students are often required to take. These basic survey courses, be they in Bible, church history, theology, religious studies, or pastoral care, have in common the difficulty of capturing the essence

---

*QR code URL: http://www.doe.in.gov/sites/default/files/cte/ncteb-edphil.pdf

of a large body of content in a semester- or quarter-long format, when this may be the only class that students take in this subject area. The temptation is to try to cover it all and rely primarily on semantic memory, using a format of lectures and quizzes or exams to test content knowledge. The problem that Inglis raises for us in her fourth chapter on "How Memory Works" is that semantic memory is the least durable and sticky. So, facts and figures that are memorized for an exam are forgotten quickly, as the next set of content comes into view.

Therefore, I would like to take you on a risky journey of reimagining what a basic course design might look like, if learning rather than teaching were the focus. The course I will use as an exemplar is our basic Christian-education course, which has been required of all Masters of Divinity students at Columbia Theological Seminary. In our new curriculum revision, this course will become one of several options for these students but required of our Master of Arts in Practical Theology students who are specializing in Christian education. My hope is that regardless of your discipline, you will be able to see connections with your own basic course planning.

This course was already in the curriculum when I arrived at the seminary in 2004. At that time, it required ten textbooks, some of which were only used for one class session. As one who came in with a background in Howard Gardner's Multiple Intelligences Theory, which Inglis summarizes above, this felt like an overemphasis on linguistic intelligence, as well as being simply too many different texts to address in any depth in the course of a twelve-week semester. Over the years, I was able gradually to reduce this to five books and in the last few years the readings have become a flexible, electronic course pack of current articles and Web resources. There is still significant content for reading, but the reading is focused on particular questions that are present in student experience and ministry settings.

Class Goals

Before making decisions about specific content to be addressed in any course, I first need to determine what the aim and goals are for this course. I have found David Perkins's work on "Teaching for Understanding" particularly helpful in this regard.[1] As a colleague of Howard Gardner and others at the Harvard Graduate School of Education, Perkins is especially attentive to much of the learning theory detailed in chapter 2 above, on "The Nature of Learning." He lifts up the importance of generative topics or throughline questions for course planning. For Perkins, these topics or overarching questions have four characteristics:

1. Central to a given discipline or subject area,

2. Connect readily to what is familiar to students, and to other subject matters,

---

1. For more information on "Teaching for Understanding," see http://www.exploratorium.edu/ifi/resources/workshops/teachingforunderstanding.html.

3. Engaging to students and to teachers,

4. Accessible to students via multiple resources and ways of thinking.[2]

I prefer questions rather than generative topics as they keep the learning more dialogical rather than teacher-centered.

Over the years, I have chosen different throughline questions to aid content selection, structure the course topics, guide class conversations over the semester, and to give us a focal point to which to return, if we stray too far off topic. These questions need to be robust enough to have multifaceted entry points and to hold student interest. Some of the ones I have used for this course in different years are: "What is the relationship between schooling and Christian education?," "What models of teaching and learning are most effective and theologically sound in growing Christian faith?," and "What is the relationship between Christian education and spiritual formation?"

Once the throughline question is set, it is important to turn to the student learning outcomes. What does the instructor want students to take away at the end of the semester that they can use in their daily lives and ministry? What skills will they need to have? How will they synthesize the material and creatively appropriate it for their own contexts? The focus here is not on the content to be communicated, but on what the learners will do and what will remain sticky for them beyond the time frame of the course itself. These fundamental questions will be addressed in greater detail as we look at class structure and assessment, but for now, let me just list some of my hopes for student learning in this course as examples. My hope is that students will leave this class being able to write a solid lesson plan to both guide their own teaching and to provide guidance for volunteer teachers they may encounter. I also want them to be able to evaluate resources from theological, developmental, educational, and practical considerations, so that they recognize quality teaching and learning helps when they encounter them. I want them to develop confidence in their own teaching skills and to discover their particular voice and rationale for educational choices they make in their ministry settings. Finally, I want them to be able to articulate clearly their own theological grounding and commitments to teaching and learning. What are your hopes for your students in the basic classes that you teach?

Once the throughline question and goals are in place, it is time to select the readings and texts that will enhance this. Here again, with the focus on student learning versus teaching, which texts are chosen and how many pages the students will read will have an impact. When viewed from a teaching perspective, professors would certainly choose their favorite texts that best communicate the theology, philosophy, and methods they hope to instill in their students. When viewing this from a student-learning perspective, one has to ask what is most needed by students now and in their future ministry. What readings do I have that can succinctly capture this information, knowing that I can't cover it all nor should I try to? My rule of

---

2. The ch. 7 QR code URL points you to Perkins's Website, which includes this list of "generative topics" as well as other aspects of the "Teaching for Understanding" framework: http://www.uknow.gse .harvard.edu/teaching/TC3-1.html.

thumb has been no more than fifty pages of reading for any class period, less if I can find the right sources. This may seem small to some and a lot for others, but with multiple professors requiring copious amounts of reading, it is faulty to assume that students are taking massive amounts of words into their semantic memory. So I tend to pair shorter readings with online media that enhances this learning. I look for provocative short articles, pithy chapters within books, or condensations of larger works that will provoke us to delve deeply into particular important topics rather than trying to go more broadly, as in a survey approach. This is especially true in the broad introductory courses. I want to whet the student's appetites to explore more from authors to whom they connect rather than to overwhelm them with too much information. I'm hoping to set them up for lifelong learning rather than to squelch their natural curiosity.

How does this method of course design relate to the learning theory and brain research that Inglis leads us to in her writing? Similar to the quotation that she gives from Eric Mazur, this method of course design is more interested in helping students learn than in communicating particular content. It focuses on real-life issues and goals that will benefit students beyond the classroom. As she states in her discussion of brain anatomy, "the reason we learn is to make meaning and order out of our experiences"—thus the throughline questions, learning goals, and readings tie back into the context from which the learner comes and the ministry to which he or she may be heading. If you're interested in seeing an actual syllabus for one of the previous iterations of this course, I provide one at the end of this response. In the narrative that follows we'll see how this course design plays out in terms of class structure and assessment.

Class Structure

Now that the course has a focus and some learning goals, it's time to think about what will actually happen during a typical class period. The basic introductory Christian-education course has been taught in two formats. Most frequently, it has occurred two mornings a week for one-and-a-half hours at each sitting. Less frequently, the class has been taught in a three-hour block format, once a week in the afternoon or evening. Is one format more helpful for long-term stickiness than another? It all depends on how the class time is structured.

When you walk into the class, many of John Medina's brain rules that Inglis enumerates are evident in either format. Hospitality is shown by providing at least beverages, if not food as well, to ensure that hunger and thirst do not detract from class participation. With the longer three-hour format, the class signs up for snack contributions at the beginning of the semester, so all contribute to the well-being of the whole.

Multiple pathways are used for engaging the topic of the day and often begin as the student enters the room. So, one may hear music playing related to the day's theme. Sometimes, interactive tasks to engage are posted on the walls of the classroom before one takes a seat. If a PowerPoint or outline is being used for a lecture portion, it is posted on the course Website before the class begins so that students have some knowledge of the class agenda for the day. This information is often communicated through a class email a day before the class meets for added preparation time. As Columbia moves more deeply into technology, this same pre-class engagement may be communicated through short digital movies made by the instructor. The important part is that there are a variety of ways that learning may commence for the student before the actual class session begins.

The space itself also communicates what will be learned and what methods might be utilized. Many seminary and university classrooms have their furnishings set up in lecture-hall fashion by default. This communicates that the information will be delivered from the teacher or media to the student in a one-way fashion, with a possible time for questions and answers directed between teacher and learner. If one is going to take Lev Vygotsky's work on the importance of collaborative peer learning seriously, as Inglis suggests in her chapter on learning theory, the configuration of classroom space itself is going to need to change. Our registrar knows that my classes need to be scheduled in flat and flexible spaces with movable tables and chairs. We will often find ourselves in small groups, a large square, learning centers, or some other configuration that lends itself to movement within the classroom. The most critical factor for me is matching the space and teaching methods utilized to the content of the class. Thus, if our topic is developing critical-thinking questions for small-group discussion, this won't be done in a lecture-hall set-up, but within small groups where questions are formulated and perhaps passed to another small group for answers and evaluation. We also don't confine our learning to the classroom, but will move to other places either on- or off-campus to tap into the episodic memory that Inglis mentions. Being in the setting most conducive for learning a particular topic will make that topic more memorable than simply being talked about in the familiar classroom where the class ordinarily meets.

Small-Group Strategies

In the last paragraph I mentioned the importance of small groups for learning. This taps into the peer coaching that Inglis mentions when she speaks of the work of Lev Vygotsky and others. There are many different ways to set these small groups. For some classes, where there is not a specific end product or performance for which the group is responsible, I sort these groups randomly and change them up throughout the semester so class participants are involved in a wide array of conversations. For the course that we are looking at in this essay, that is not the case. These small groups will be responsible for a group lesson to which all must contribute, so there needs to be a certain amount of group bonding and cohesiveness throughout the semester.

In setting up these groups, I am intentional about having a variety of ages, levels of experience, and diversity in cultural and denominational backgrounds. This will inevitably result in some conflict, but also greater learning over the course of the semester. On the second day of class, a writing assignment is due where each student talks about his or her Christian-education experience as both a learner and leader. These essays give me some basis for setting up the groups and also alert me to particular experiences that may lend themselves to topics we will be addressing. For instance, one year I discovered that one of the students had a great deal of training and experience in a particular adult intensive Bible-study system. When we were addressing adult education in the church, I invited her to share her experience with the class and lead us in a sample lesson from this series. So, the essays have purposes beyond the setting of small groups, but that is certainly one of their primary functions.

Once the groups are formed, with all their diversity, we talk about the life cycle of small groups and some of the needed roles to help them function effectively. "Life-cycle" terminology is based on the work of Bruce Tuckman from the 1960s, but still has value today. In this view of the small group, most groups cycle in and out of certain stages of performance. These are termed "forming, storming, norming, performing, and adjourning or mourning," when the group reaches the end of its work together. This again relates back to the collaborative-learning theory addressed earlier in this book. Not every class period is set in small groups (see spatial issues above), but in the three-hour format of this class, these groups often function in the last hour of the class to teach a group lesson on the topic of the day and thus increase the student learning on the topic, through leadership and participation with their peers.

A good source for the definitions of these stages and important group roles of individual members can be found here.[3]

One last issue concerning small groups at Columbia—our student body is increasingly more diverse racially, culturally, and theologically. Much of the literature on group dynamics and functioning is written from a white Western mindset, so as instructor, I am constantly looking for differing ways of functioning in a group setting. We look at base-community Bible studies from Central and South America. We try on the group dynamics of the Mutual Invitation Model, developed by Eric Law for multicultural settings and other such non-Western ways of being together. By the performing stage, which will occur at different times for different groups, the group should be able to execute a group lesson, where each member has a voice and participates.

This group lesson uses the existing members of the class as the proposed audience. The groups are not teaching in a mock setting, with ages other than adults, or in settings other than the seminary environment. Rather, contextualization happens through the individual lesson plans and the presentation that each student will do in her or his own church or other ministry setting. When the class size is less than twenty, I visit each site as part of the process. This attention to context

---

3. QR code URL: http://www.skillsyouneed.com/ips/group-life-cycle.html.

benefits not only the students, who are faced with real-life dilemmas and changes of scheduling, but also benefits me, as instructor, because it helps me to contextualize the learning that happens in the classroom as well. Inglis mentions that we usually teach from our own educational experience, so observing students in different contexts helps me to expand my own norms of ministry by broadening my field of vision from the churches and ministries of which I have been a part. Some students have chosen to do their teaching in house churches, campus-ministry settings, or in prisons, so the teaching definitely takes on the flavor of each context and audience to which it is addressed.

Large-Class Strategies

I mentioned that this is the plan when the class size is fewer than twenty. Any more than this presents difficulties in instructor time and sanity, even when doing some of this instruction via filmed lessons rather than being present in body. For larger classes, I rely more on peer review of the lesson plans and extensive reflection on teaching by the person presenting the lesson. Each student gets multiple feedbacks to improve their individual teaching at various stages of the assignment. This will become clearer in the assessment portion of this response.

So, overall, class time is spent in short presentations, interactive and experiential forms for learning the material, class discussions and projects, and group lessons. Each of these taps into multiple entry points to make memories stick and relies on different learning styles and intelligences. By changing up the class time each week, I'm also ensuring that the models that these students receive for their own teaching are varied. So, when they enter their own teaching settings, they won't be reliant on only one particular way of enhancing learning. For some who thrive in the lecture model, this is a frustrating experience, at least initially, but usually part way through the semester they begin to see how their classmates are responding to different forms of teaching and learning, realizing that we all learn differently and that if we want to enhance the learning of others versus communicating information, we sometimes have to teach in ways in which we ourselves do not learn as well.

Going from the class session to assessing learning is our last movement in this chapter. Given that we are teaching in academic institutions, grading in some shape or form is a mandate. In this next section, we'll look at the ways that both course participation and group and individual learning are assessed in this particular class.

Assessment

Assessment comes in many varieties, although you may not realize this to look at some courses in theological education. There is *summative assessment*, which often happens in the middle and at the end of courses, when the teacher is trying to ascertain how much of the communicated body of knowledge has been retained. This is most often accomplished through examinations or final papers. There is also *formative assessment*, which often happens continually, where students receive feedback about their mastery of a specific skill or are given comments on a draft, which will lead to an eventual summative product that will be graded. This latter approach seems much more in line with best practices in assessment in sticky learning as Inglis outlines toward the end of her writing. It is also aligned with my own view that assessment continues the learning rather than being an ending punctuation mark at the conclusion of a course.

For this course, a number of these formative assignments lead to sticky learning. The first is actually the course-participation grade. In this course, it is worth 20 percent of the total grade. There are many times that the students are engaged in learning in class that is ungraded, yet requires preparation and participation. Yes, it is somewhat subjective, as compared to a multiple-choice quiz or a reading review paper, but there is a set of criteria or rubric that the syllabus lists to guide this evaluation. The criteria are as follows: "regular attendance, punctuality, contributions to class/small-group discussion, citations of reading in discussions, engagement in interactive experiences, and small-group tasks." This helps the learner to see that simply being a warm body in the room is not sufficient to succeed in this grading category. It also invites the student into a deeper engagement with the material by encouraging him or her to participate in the variety of activities set up during the class time to make the learning stick.

From course participation, we move to the initial assignment mentioned in the section above regarding the formation of small groups. This is a reflection paper on their Christian-education experience, centered on two questions: "What have been your experiences of Christian education? What have those experiences meant to you and your faith formation?" This two- to three-page assignment, worth 10 percent of the grade, is due the second class session. For grading purposes, its sole criteria is completion by the due date, but it serves many formative purposes beyond this. It is a help to the formation of small groups and alerts the instructor to levels of experience within Christian education and particular knowledge and skills that may be woven into the course. Beyond these things, this assignment also helps me to see how the students are defining "Christian education" and "faith formation," key terms within this field of study. For some, their initial definitions are very narrow in setting, audience, and content. For others, who may be adult converts, there is very little experience with the terminology and they have no frame of reference to answer the questions. This is helpful information to have as an instructor as we embark upon our semester together.

Early on in the semester, the students are instructed in how to write a lesson plan. Mastery of this craft is one of the tangible student-learning outcomes for this course. They will have two experiences with formative assessments along the way for practicing this skill. One is individual and one is related to their small group. The in-class implementation of these assignments has been discussed above, but the sequence and assessment of these lesson plans and teaching have not, and that is what will be the focus in this section.

Both assignments begin with the same early lesson that walks through the lesson-plan format used at the seminary—a standard five-step lesson plan that can be adapted as needed for different teaching methods. This class period involves different interactive games along the way to make the learning sticky. Even so, it may be several months before some students actually try to write their individual or group lesson plan, so I have also recorded an audio PowerPoint version of the same information that is available on our course site to reinforce the learning and as review.

When the student is ready to write their lesson plan for their individual teaching in a setting that they know well, they turn in a draft of their lesson plan, one week before they teach it. This is to give the instructor time for comments before the lesson is actually taught. Part of this lesson-plan outline is to develop a rationale for the decisions they make along the way. This is two to three pages of speaking about why they chose the topic for their chosen students, how the topic and lesson sequence relates to the developmental level of their students, what choices they have made regarding teaching methodology, development of discussion questions, and learning objectives or outcomes, relating these things to the course readings we have been addressing in class. This added piece, which would not ordinarily be handed to another teacher with the plan, allows me to see their reasoning before they teach.

After they receive these initial comments from the instructor, several days before the teaching session, they can make any changes they deem necessary in their plan before actually teaching it. If the instructor is able to be present for the lesson taught, the student receives additional comments about their actual teaching, both what went well from the observer's standpoint and areas for improvement. Whether the instructor is present or not, the student writes up his or her own reflection on the teaching moment. The assessment criteria on this assignment are not that they have a perfect plan and execution, but that they have a clear reason for why they are doing what they do in the classroom and that they are able to reflect and grow from the experience. When the instructor does not visit the teaching sites, the last part of this assessment is uploading their final lesson plans with rationale and teaching reflection to a discussion forum or blog for their small group and getting some peer comments as well as final instructor comments on their experience. It is only at this point that the instructor communicates the final summative grade for the assignment to the individual student. So as you can see, there is much formative assessment by multiple individuals before the final evaluation for the grade. This is another hallmark of sticky assessment.

With the group lessons, the initial process is similar to the individual lessons, with the same class session on lesson-plan writing, the lesson outline being due a week before teaching, and the initial instructor comments on their draft plan. Beyond this, there are several differences. Writing the lesson plan as a group brings in more of the group dynamics mentioned above and often leads to storming, as competing ideas for implementation are offered. Usually, the instructor will listen to these conflicts, but encourages the group to continue to try to work out a solution on their own usually thorough consensus, where each group member is still engaged and participating. This is also part of the learning for this assignment.

There is also a group-feedback mechanism, when the group lesson is presented during the class period. Those students who are not members of the group that is teaching are asked to fill out half-sheets on which they are invited to try to identify what the goal of the lesson might have been on the lesson plan (which they have not seen), and to give both affirmations and constructive helps on the teaching they have experienced. The writers of these evaluation sheets voice some of these latter comments to the group, so the group gets some immediate feedback on their lesson. The papers are then collected and integrated into the instructor's comments to the group, before being returned to the group for their edification. I try to do this on the same day that the lesson occurs or the next day, so that the lesson is still fresh in their minds. I communicate my comments via a group email to the small group who has taught. This gives the class ownership to the assignment and ensures that each group will be hearing multiple perspectives on their teaching. It also reinforces that not everyone learns in the same way, so others will affirm different elements of the lesson that didn't connect with other students.

Finally, there is a one-page paper assignment that asks students to summarize succinctly their theology of Christian education. This is done in draft form midway through the course and then finalized by the end of the course. Why is this only one page? Even though this is a basic course in Christian education, its sequence in our curriculum up until this year has been in the third of the three years of the MDiv-degree program. Due to the timing of this course, many of the students are preparing materials for interviews with churches or higher governing bodies. A succinct statement of their theology of Christian education may serve them well in such settings, both as a verbal response and something that could form a portfolio of samples of ministry that could be passed on to a calling committee.

To make this assignment cohesive and focused, each student is encouraged to choose either a passage of Scripture, theological doctrine, or sacramental idea to serve as the basis of their statement. Frequent choices have been Matthew 28:19-20, Deuteronomy 6:4-9, and baptism. Even so, I am always amazed by the diversity, creativity, and depth of these assignments and the many ways that our faith speaks to educational ministry. By the time this statement is finalized for purposes of this class, it will also be heavily cited as the students link their own beliefs to the course readings we have experienced together. These citations often cause the statement to spill over into a second page, but the body is still succinct and can be used in other settings, as noted before.

Again, this is a formative assignment because of the feature of drafting before finalizing and having multiple points of contact with the instructor. These, too, are used in the small-group setting in their final form, as each small group tries to craft a theological statement that incorporates some of the ideas of each of their members. This is modeling an activity that then can be translated to a Christian-education committee or anytime a group is settling in to create an educational event or write curriculum for others.

The hallmark of each of these assessment artifacts is that they have a purpose rooted and grounded in the experience of the learners and they have implications for continued learning beyond the length of the course itself. I'm not sure that the same thing can be said about summative assessments that focus on short-term memory of a particular body of knowledge that spills forth in an examination period. As an instructor and a curator of learning, I'm not particularly interested in that type of assessment, but in planting the seeds that I may not be present to see come to fruition. I want to inspire a hunger for learning that sticks and grows in service of our one master teacher, who continues to work within us toward the same purpose.

Sample Syllabus

P322—Introduction to the Theory and Practice of Christian Education

Course Description:

This course examines the possible relations between our understandings of God, mission, and education in today's church. Students analyze selected contemporary educational theories and practices, become familiar with basic educational concepts, and begin to develop their own practical approaches as practical theologians to Christian religious education in the church.

Guiding Question for the Course:

What models of teaching and learning are most effective and theologically sound in growing Christian faith?

Goals for the Course:

Given the class sessions, readings, and assignments, by the end of the course, the learner will:

1. Understand the theories and decision-making practices that are implicit in the writing of lesson plans (both individually and in small groups) for particular age groups.

2. Understand what education in the church is called to be through the writings of Foster, Harris, Wimberly, Fowler, Palmer, Bass, Volf, and others.

3. Integrate previous experience and course readings into developing an emerging theology of Christian education for ministry.

4. Develop Christian-education skills such as: analyzing resources, writing a lesson plan, leading a discussion, planning and assessing programs/events, and collaborating in a small group.

Required Online Reader (also available on reserve in the library). No more than one chapter/article from the following that are print resources:
@This Point, Spring 2010 issue, http://www.atthispoint.net.
Bass, Dorothy, and Miroslav Volf, eds. *Practicing Theology: Beliefs and Practices in Christian Life*. Grand Rapids: Eerdmans, 2002.

Beckwith, Ivy. *Postmodern Children's Ministry: Ministry to Children in the Twenty-First Century*. Grand Rapids: Zondervan, 2004.

Berryman, Jerome W. *The Complete Guide to Godly Play, vol. 1: How to Lead Godly Play Lessons*. Denver: Living the Good News, 2002.

Corbitt, J. Nathan, and Vivian Nix-Early. *Taking It to the Streets: Using the Arts to Transform Your Community*. Grand Rapids: Baker, 2003.

Dean, Kenda Creasy, and Ron Foster. *The Godbearing Life: The Art of Soul Tending for Youth Ministry*. Nashville: Upper Room, 1998.

Foster, Charles R. *Educating Congregations: The Future of Christian Education*. Nashville: Abingdon, 1994.

Fowler, James, and Mary Lynn Dell. "Stages of Faith from Infancy through Adolescence: Reflections on Three Decades of Faith Development Theory." In Eugene C. Roehlkepartain, et al., eds., *The Handbook of Spiritual Development in Childhood and Adolescence*, 34–45. Thousand Oaks, CA: Sage, 2006.

Freire, Paulo. *Teachers as Cultural Workers: Letters to Those Who Dare to Teach*. Trans. Donald Amcedo, Dale Koike, and Alexandre Oliveira. Boulder: Westview, 1998.

Gardner, Howard. *Intelligence Reframed: Multiple Intelligences for the Twenty-First Century*. New York: Basic, 1999.

Griggs, Donald L. *Teaching Today's Teachers to Teach*. Nashville: Abingdon, 2003.

Harris, Maria. *Fashion Me a People: Curriculum in the Church*. Louisville: Westminster John Knox, 1989.

Hess, Mary. "What Difference Does It Make? E-Learning and Faith Community." *Word & World* 30, no. 3 (Summer 2010): 281–90.

Hill, Andrea, Tammi Arford, Amy Lubitow, and Leandra M. Smollin. "I'm Ambivalent about it": The Dilemmas of PowerPoint." *Teaching Sociology* 40 (2012): 242–56.

Hymans, Diane J. "Education and Evangelism: Is the Connection Essential?" In Norma Cook Everist, ed., *Christian Education as Evangelism*, 11–21. Minneapolis: Fortress Press, 2007.

Law, Eric H. F. *The Wolf Shall Dwell with the Lamb: A Spirituality for Leadership in a Multicultural Community*. St. Louis: Chalice, 1993.

Medina, John. *Brain Rules: Twelve Principles for Surviving and Thriving at Work, Home, and School*. Seattle: Pear Press, 2008.

Noddings, Nel. "The Aims of Education." In David J. Flinders and Stephen J. Thornton, eds., *The Curriculum Studies Reader*, 2d ed., 163–70, New York: RoutledgeFalmer, 2004.

Osmer, Richard Robert. *Teaching for Faith: A Guide for Teachers of Adult Classes*. Louisville: Westminster John Knox, 1992.

Palmer, Parker. *The Courage to Teach: Exploring the Inner Landscape of a Teacher's Life*. San Francisco: Jossey-Bass, 1998.

Smith, Christian, with Melinda Lundquist Denton. *Soul Searching: The Religious and Spiritual Lives of American Teenagers*. New York: Oxford University Press, 2005.

Vann, Jane Rogers. *Gathered before God: Worship-Centered Church Renewal*. Louisville: Westminster John Knox, 2004.

Wimberly, Anne Streaty. *Soul Stories: African American Christian Education*. Nashville: Abingdon, 1994.

Course Requirements:

1. *Class attendance and participation.* If you must miss class, please let the professor and your small group know, if possible, ahead of time, preferably by email.

2. *Preparation for class.* Please do the reading and come ready to discuss the text and ask questions, etc.

3. *Description/reflection paper on your experience of Christian education.* Due on **Monday, Sept. 10,** this is a description of your Christian-education experiences and a reflection upon those experiences. (2–3 pages) Address the following questions:

   – What have been your experiences of Christian education?

   – What have those experiences meant to you and your faith formation?

4. *Theology of Christian education.* First draft is due on **Thursday, October 11,** final draft on **Thursday, November 29.** This is meant to be a continuous task (indeed, lifelong!). Think about choosing one Scripture, theological doctrine, or sacramental notion that might form the basis of your statement. Write on ONE PAGE the body of your theology of Christian education (double-spaced, standard margins, 12 point font, no cover page). Craft this for your average lay member or Pastor Nominating Committee (PNC). It is expected that you will use footnotes/endnotes from the readings that match or contrast with your ideas. These do not count into the one-page stipulation.

5. *Group lesson plan and presentation:* Each small group will present a **30-minute** lesson designed to teach a Scripture passage or Christian practice in a way that is appropriate to the content of the models for that day. Groups should turn in their aims/goals for the lesson and an appropriate outline/plan for the teaching they will be doing **one week** before the lesson is presented.

6. *Solo lesson plan and presentation.* Each student will prepare a lesson plan for use in a particular teaching setting in a congregation or agency. The professor will provide models for the lesson plan, including its required components. (See Sept. 13 class session, below). **A first draft of the lesson plan is due no later than one week before you present it.** The final version of the lesson plan is due no later than Thursday, December 5, although it may be turned in as soon as you have revised your lesson plan in light of the comments you've received and created a blog within our

course site reflecting on your teaching. Your solo teaching is scheduled outside of class times at a location and with an audience of your choice.

Grading:

- Class attendance, participation, preparation: 20% (regular attendance, punctuality, contributions to class/small-group discussion, citations of reading in discussions, engagement in interactive experiences and small-group tasks).
- Reflection paper: 10% (completion)
- Theology statement: 20% (understandability, depth, integration of readings, lectures, discussions, consistency, and coherence)
- Group lesson plan and presentation: 25% (content matches process, written plan leads to replication, creativity, active participation of the whole team, active participation of the learners, peer reviews)
- Solo lesson plan and presentation: 25% (quality of writing, clarity of ideas, creativity, active participation of the learners, evidence of integration of developmental and teaching and learning theories—e.g., Osmer's structure for questions, etc.—clarity of presentation and reflection blog).

Note: Ordinarily, late assignments will be reduced one grade per class the assignment is late.

CAMS Default Grading Scale
A = 94–100 points
A- = 90–93 points
B+ = 87–89 points
B = 84–86 points
B- = 80–83 points
C+ = 77–79 points
C = 74–76 points
C- = 70–73 points
D = 60–69 points
F = 20–59 points

Table 8.1

Course Schedule:

Date	Topic	Reading	Assignment
Thurs. Sept. 6	Introductory Matters: Including definitions and aims of Christian education	Hymans and Noddings readings	
Thurs. Sept. 13	The Art of Lesson-Plan Writing	@This Point and Griggs readings	Description/reflection paper on Christian-education experience due on **Monday,** Sept. 10
Thurs. Sept. 20	Minding the Learner	Fowler reading and Gardner Webinar	
Thurs. Sept. 27	Minding the Teacher	Palmer reading, Freire letter, and Opening Doors to Discipleship Website	
Thurs. Oct. 4	Models for Children	Berryman and Beckwith readings	Group Lesson
Thurs. Oct. 11	Models for Youth	Dean and Smith readings	Draft of Theology Statement Due Group Lesson
Thurs. Oct. 18	Models for Adults	Medina, Bass & Dykstra readings	Group Lesson
Midterm Assessment Week			
Thurs. Nov. 1	Models for Intergenerational Learning	Wimberly, ANA Multiple Generations, and Vann readings	Group Lesson
Thurs. Nov. 8	Models for Using Technology	Hill and Hess readings	Group Lesson
Thurs. Nov. 15	Models That Inspire Discussion	Osmer and Law readings, Collaborative Learning Webinar	Group Lesson
Thanksgiving Break			
Thurs. Nov. 29	Models That Incorporate the Arts	Foster and Corbitt & Nix-Early readings	Final Draft of Theology Statement Due Group Lesson
Thurs. Dec. 5	Planning the Curriculum of the Church	Harris and Planning Guide readings	

Works Cited

Ambrose, Susan A., et al. *How Learning Works: Seven Research-Based Principles for Smart Teaching.* San Francisco: Jossey-Bass, 2010.

Arnett, Jeffrey Jensen, and Jennifer Lynn Tanner. *Emerging Adults in America: Coming of Age in the Twenty-First Century.* Washington, DC: American Psychological Association, 2006.

Association of Theological Schools. "Annual Institutional Data Tables: Table 2.14-B Head Count Enrollment by Degree Program, Age, and Gender, Fall 2012." http://www.ats.edu/uploads/resources/institutional-data/annual-data-tables/2012-2013-annual-data-tables.pdf.

Atkins, Peter. *Memory and Liturgy.* Brookfield, VT: Ashgate, 2004.

Barr, Robert B., and John Tagg. "From Teaching to Learning—A New Paradigm for Undergraduate Education." *Change* (November/December 1995): 13–25.

Blackwood, Rick. *The Power of Multi-Sensory Preaching and Teaching.* Grand Rapids: Zondervan, 2008.

Bruce, Barbara. *Our Spiritual Brain.* Nashville: Abingdon, 2002.

Caine, Renate Nummela, and Geoffrey Caine. *Making Connections: Teaching and the Human Brain.* Alexandria, VA: Association for Supervision and Curriculum Development, 1991.

Calvin, John. *Institutes of the Christian Religion.* Trans. Henry Beveridge. Grand Rapids: Eerdmans, 1994.

Dell'Olio, Jeanine M., and Tony Donk. *Models of Teaching: Connecting Student Learning with Standards.* Thousand Oaks, CA: Sage, 2007.

Dewey, John. *Democracy and Education* (19). New York: Macmillan, 1916. Quoted in Thomas H. Groome, *Christian Religious Education.* San Francisco: Jossey-Bass, 1980.

Doll, William E. "The Four R's—An Alternative to the Tyler Rationale." In David J. Flinders and Stephen J. Thornton, eds., *The Curriculum Studies Reader*, 2d ed., 255–56. New York: RoutledgeFalmer, 2004.

Foer, Joshua. "Remember This." *National Geographic* (November 2007): 32–55.

Gardner, Howard. *Frames of Mind: The Theory of Multiple Intelligences.* New York: Basic Books, 1983.

———. *Five Minds for the Future.* Boston: Harvard Business Press, 2008.

Gathercole, Susan E., and Tracey Packiam Alloway. *Working Memory and Learning.* Thousand Oaks, CA: Sage, 2008.

Gladwell, Malcolm. *The Tipping Point: How Little Things Can Make a Big Difference.* New York: Little, Brown, 2000.

Griffiths, Sarah. "Your Brain Really IS Faster than You Think." *Mail Online.* http://www.dailymail.co.uk/sciencetech/article-2542583/Scientists-record-fastest-time-human-image-takes-just-13-milliseconds.html.

Hart, Leslie A. *Human Brain and Human Learning.* New York: Longman, 1983.

Heath, Chip, and Dan Heath. *Made to Stick.* New York: Random House, 2007.

Hogue, David A. *Remembering the Future, Imagining the Past: Story, Ritual, and the Human Brain*. Cleveland: Pilgrim, 2003.

Inglis, Holly. "Hearers and Doers: Becoming a Whole-Brain Church." D. Ed. Min. thesis, Columbia Theological Seminary, 2012.

Jackson, Michelle. "Prior Knowledge Check." BYU Center for Teaching and Learning. http://ctl.byu.edu/teaching-tips/prior-knowledge-check.

Jensen, Eric. *Brain-Based Learning*. Thousand Oaks, CA: Corwin, 2008.

———. *Teaching with the Brain in Mind*. 2d ed. Alexandria, Va.: Association for Supervision and Curriculum Development, 2005.

———. *Introduction to Brain-Compatible Learning*. San Diego: The Brain Store, 1998.

Kelly, Rob. "Six Ways to Support Adult Online Learners." *Faculty Focus*. http://www.facultyfocus.com/articles/online-education/six-ways-to-support-adult-online-learners/.

Kramer, A. F., et al. "Aging, Fitness and Neurocognitive Function." *Nature* 400 (July 1999): 418–19.

Lambert, Craig. "Twilight of the Lecture." *Harvard Magazine*. March-April 2012. http://harvardmagazine.com/2012/03/twilight-of-the-lecture.

Larsen, Jerry. *Religious Education and the Brain*. Mahwah, NJ: Paulist, 2000.

LeDoux, Joseph E.. "The Emotional Brain, Fear, and the Amygdala." *Cellular and Molecular Neurobiology* 23, nos. 4/5 (October 2003): 727–38.

———. "Emotion, Memory, and the Brain." *Scientific American* 220 (June 1994): 50–57.

McGaugh, James L. "Memory Consolidation and the Amygdala." In *Modern Brains: Enhancing Memory and Performance in This Distracting Digital Age*, 301-306. Conference proceedings: Learning and the Brain Conference. Boston: Public Information Resources, 2009.

Medina, John. *Brain Rules*. Seattle: Pear Press, 2008.

———. "12 Brain Rules—Illustrated." *Brain Rules*. http://www.brainrules.net/the-rules.

Palmer, Parker. *The Courage To Teach*. San Francisco: Jossey-Bass, 1998.

———. "Good Teaching: A Matter of Living the Mystery." *Center for Courage & Renewal*. http://www.couragerenewal.org/parker/writings/good-teaching/.

Paul, Marla. "Your Memory is Like the Telephone Game." Northwestern University. http://www.northwestern.edu/newscenter/stories/2012/09/your-memory-is-like-the-telephone-game.html.

Perkins, David, and Tina Blythe. "What Is Teaching for Understanding?" Harvard Graduate School of Education. http://www.uknow.gse.harvard.edu/teaching/TC3-1.html.

Prieto, Nicklas. "Debunking the Myth of Multitasking at the Office." Docstoc.com. http://www.docstoc.com/article/168729842/Debunking-the-Myth-of-Multitasking-at-the-Office.

Ratey, John J., and Eric Hagerman. *Spark: the Revolutionary New Science of Exercise and the Brain*. New York: Little, Brown, 2008.

Realization^{SM}. "Realization—The Effects of Multitasking on Organizations." *Realization*. http://www.realization.com/the-effects-of-multitasking-on-organizations.

Shimron, Yonat. "Seminaries Continue to Attract Older Students." *Insights into Religion*. http://religioninsights.org/articles/seminaries-continue-attract-older-students.

Sprenger, Marilee. *Learning and Memory: The Brain in Action*. Alexandria, VA: Association for Supervision and Curriculum Development, 1999.

Vygotsky, L. S.. *Mind in Society*. Ed. Vera John-Steiner, Sylvia Scribner, Ellen Souberman, Michael Cole. Cambridge: Harvard University Press, 1978.

———. *The Collected Words of L.S. Vygotsky. Volume 2: The Fundamentals of Defectology*. Ed. R. W. Rieber and A. S. Carton. Trans. J. E. Knos and C. B. Stevens. New York: Plenum, 1993.

Wheeler, Barbara G., Anthony T. Ruger, and Sharon L. Miller. "Students and Graduates: Theological Student Enrollment." Auburn Seminary. http://www.auburnseminary.org /students-and-graduates?par=838.

Willis, Judy. "The Neuroscience and Strategies for Maximizing Children's Long-term Memory and Brain Potential." In *Modern Brains: Enhancing Memory and Performance in This Distracting Digital Age*, 103–113. Conference proceedings: Learning and the Brain Conference. Boston: Public Information Resources, 2009.

Wimberly, Anne Streaty. *Soul Stories: African American Christian Education*. Nashville: Abingdon, 1994.

Wolfe, Pat. "The Adolescent Brain: A Work in Progress." *Mind Matters, Inc.* http://patwolfe .com/2011/09/the-adolescent-brain-a-work-in-progress/.

Wood, Willy. "Seven Steps to Magical Memory." In *Modern Brains: Enhancing Memory and Performance in This Distracting Digital Age*, 347–53. Conference proceedings: Learning and the Brain Conference. Boston: Public Information Resources, 2009.

Zull, James. *The Art of Changing the Brain*. Sterling, VA: Stylus, 2002.

———. "Key Aspects of How the Brain Learns." *New Directions for Adult and Continuing Education* 110 (Summer 2006): 3–9.